KNEELING BESIDE DANTE

A RENAISSANCE

OF THE ROMANTIC

IN POETRY AND ART

Cover Art

Dante and Beatrice, c.1916-17 (oil on canvas)

John William Waterhouse (1849-1917)

The Bridgeman Art Library

KNEELING BESIDE DANTE

A RENAISSANCE
OF THE ROMANTIC
IN POETRY AND ART

A Poetry Collection

by

Patricia Anne Kirby Craddock

An eclectic selection of poems on poetry and art,

love and faith, nature and the world,

calling for a considered contemporary *caesura*

from our

Modernist-Minimalist-Impressionist art and verse

and a rebirth, a renaissance,

of the Romantic

First Edition

Pontifex Press, LLC
Atlanta, Georgia

Pontifex Press, LLC
Atlanta, GA

Published in 2014 by Pontifex Press, LLC.
Distributed to the trade by Lulu Press, Inc.

ISBN-10: 0-9913009-2-0
ISBN-13: 978-0-9913009-2-1

Visit Pontifex Press's website at www.PontifexPress.com

Book design and layout by Stephanie N. Bryan

Cover Art: *Dante and Beatrice*
c.1916-17 (oil on canvas)
By John William Waterhouse (1849-1917)
Copyright © Dahesh Museum of Art, New York, USA
The Bridgeman Art Library

Back cover: Detail of a dove from a mosaic of St. Francis by Athos Menaboni, in the author's private collection

Printed in the United States of America

ACKNOWLEDGMENTS

"Advent" was published in *XXX Concorso, Centro di Cultura, Santa Croce, Taranto, Italy, in 2006.*

"Afterworld" was published in *the new renaissance*, Arlington, Massachusetts, Issue #41, Fall 2009.

"And I Am Clothed in Raiment Rare" appeared in the *American Poetry Annual,* The Amherst Society, Baltimore, Maryland, 1993.

"Annunciation" was published in *XX Concorso, Centro di Cultura, Santa Croce,* Taranto, Italy, 1988.

"Caravanserai" came out in *OggiFuturo,* Reggio Calabria, Italy, Nov.-Dec., 1998.

"Carvings" was published in *Art/Life*, Vol. 13, No. 10, Ventura, California, 1993.

"Choices" came out in the *XXIV Concorso Internazionale di Poesia Religiosa* Anthology, *Centro di Cultura, Santa Croce,* Taranto, Italy, in 2008.

"Credo" was published in *OggiFuturo*, Reggio Calabria, Italy, Jan.-Apr. 2009, and in *OggiFuturo* May-Aug. 2010 (2nd Prize *ex aequo*), and on *OggiFuturo* internet web site in 2010.

"Daughters of the Rhine at Play" appeared in the *Dan River Anthology,* Conservatory of American Letters, Thomaston, Maine, 2004.

"Earthwatch" came out in *The First Northwoods Anthology* (2004) and in *The Second Northwoods Anthology* (2005), Thomaston, Maine.

"For an Unknown Disfigured One in the Cathedral" was published in *The Cord*, The Franciscan Institute, St. Bonaventure, New York, May-June 2001.

"Fragment Preserved in Amber" appeared in *the new renaissance*, Arlington, Massachusetts, Issue #40, Fall 2008.

ACKNOWLEDGMENTS (Continued)

"Genius" came out in *Art Times*, Mt. Marion, New York, in Jan.-Feb. 2008.

"Georgia Bound" was published in *A Book of the Charter Year,* Georgia State Poetry Society, Atlanta, Georgia, 8/30/79-80, and in *Georgia State Poetry Society Newsletter*, Vol. 1, No. 3, January 1980. The poem was awarded First Place in the Ben W. Fortson, Jr., Memorial Awards, the Georgia State Poetry Society's first annual poetry Competition, January 1980.

"Gray Saturday at Oglethorpe" appeared in *The Tower*, XVI, Oglethorpe University, Atlanta, Georgia, 1985. The poem was awarded First Prize in Oglethorpe University's 150th Anniversary poetry contest.

"In Competition with Shakespeare" came out in *North American Mentor Magazine*, Fennimore, Wisconsin, in Spring 1979.

"Kneeling with Pope Julius in the Sistine Chapel" was published in the *XXX Concorso Internazionale di Poesia Religiousa* Anthology, Taranto, Italy, in 1998.

"Lines from a Poet Still in Love ... with William Shakespeare" appeared in *Art Times*, Mt. Marion, New York, in April 2008.

"Love Duet" came out in The International Library of Poetry Anthology, *The International Who's Who in Poetry,* Owings Mill, Maryland, 2005.

"Nescit Cedere" was published in the Georgia State Poetry Society volume, *The Reach of Song*, Book 3, Atlanta, Georgia, 1985. The poem was awarded First Place in the Georgia Semiquincentenary Awards (Traditional), January, 1983. It was printed in the program and read at the Oglethorpe Day Convocation at Oglethorpe University, Atlanta, February 10, 1983. In addition, it was published in *The DeKalb News Sun* newspaper, Atlanta, February 16, 1983, and in *The Flying Petrel,* Oglethorpe University, Vol. 63, No. 5, June 1983.

"On a Bus Ride to Somewhere" appeared in *The Reach of Song*, Book 2, the Georgia State Poetry Society, Atlanta, Georgia, in 1983.

ACKNOWLEDGMENTS (Continued)

"On Dante and His Language" came out in the *North American Mentor Magazine*, Fennimore, Wisconsin, in 1974.

"Poet Laureate of Ants" came out in *the new renaissance*, Arlington, Massachusetts, in Issue #41, Fall 2009.

"Requiem" was in *the new renaissance,* Arlington, Massachusetts, in Issue #40, 2008.

"The Sum of Things" was in *OggiFuturo*, Reggio Calabria, Italy, Nov.-Dec. 1998.

"To Lisa", from the author's published book-length verse-drama, *The Council of Heaven—An Allegory of Love, Human and Divine* (First Edition, Mellen Poetry Press, Lewiston, NY, 2010 and Second Edition, Pontifex Press, LLC, Atlanta, GA, 2014), initially appeared in *OggiFuturo,* Reggio Calabria, Italy, Apr.-May 2000.

DEDICATION

To my daughter,

Mimi Elizabeth Kirby Bryan:

you will understand these love songs to the world

for you have kept our feet on the ground

even when our heads were in the clouds.

"Most of the world's great art and poetry of love was produced under the inspiration of the Catholic philosophy of love. While *eros* was subordinate to charity, it could rise almost to the level of charity, ... Not so long ago, Catholics felt themselves to be part of something tremendous, a fellowship both humbling and ennobling in its vastness. The art of Europe was theirs in a special way, because it came out of that fellowship, and they felt the deep consolation of sharing a vision with geniuses as great and as disparate as Dante, Michelangelo, Shakespeare and Mozart. The esthetic reinforced the spiritual sense of communion.... The esthete may be tempted to kneel before a genius like Dante. It is the Catholic's infinitely sweeter privilege to kneel beside him."

—Joseph Sobran, from his article
"Kneeling Beside Dante"
in *Catholic eye* #28, 1/28/1986,
The National Committee of Catholic Layman, Inc.,
(Use of title and quote by Publisher's permission)

KNEELING BESIDE DANTE

Table of Contents

Table of Contents (Continued)

Table of Contents (Continued)

KNEELING BESIDE DANTE

Author's Preface

On Poetry and Art—Life Raft in a Sea of Uncertainty

Amid wars and all the other challenges to man's survival in the turbulent world of today, from Divine Providence, planetary events, and his fellow man, there is one consoling grace both spiritual and worldly, one constant, in our natural pursuit of a life well lived and loved: *Art!*

What else can so ennoble and enable us to suffer and endure, to advance from lust for war to love of peace, and ultimately to *agape*, the highest form of love for God and man? To rise to a higher plane, in the words of Nikos Kazantzakis in his novel *Saint Francis: "to transubstantiate the matter that God has entrusted to us and turn it into spirit".* The joy we find in envisioning, creating and appreciating art, whether it is the written/spoken word or works of visual art, performing arts, or other, is redemptive. From Dante and Michelangelo and Shakespeare to the moderns, via angels and saints and prophets, men mortal like ourselves have given us the sublime gift of great art. It is an unmerited earthly reward that gives us hope of Heaven, a preview of Paradise! Painting and sculpture, poetry and prose, music and dance, drama and film—there is no limit to the variations on the theme of art to enthrall and inspire us.

And what, my fellow readers, writers, artists and poets—all you creative souls—is *your* Art, your passion, your highest form of self-expressive re-creation?

Long pondering Art's influence on myself and upon those around me, I now view it as a life raft in a sea of uncertainty and anxiety. As cultural, emotional and intellectual antidotes to the ravages of war, terrorism, crime, death, mortal calamities all, afflicting human flesh and spirit. Art, both in its execution and in its veneration, has no equal, especially—and essentially—when it embodies faith in a higher power, a Supreme Being. I look upon war and the hateful atrocities committed by man against man and yet am not disheartened by failings of the individual self, but am persuaded that only the richness of love, for God and for each other, will provide answer to the poverty of compassion in our universal human condition: our inhumanity to one another.

Preface (Continued)

But how may one achieve this idealized if unrealistic goal? I wrestle like Jacob with the Angel with the reality of death in all its fateful forms, as it has touched me and must touch us all, and still I am not disillusioned with humanity or with my faith in the eventual triumph of good over evil. Instead, trembling at all the cataclysmic events terrorism and the world thrust upon us and, still, trying to return good for evil, I take pen in hand and dare to write a poem!

So I hope to add my humble but optimistic effort to the triumphant survival of civilization as we have known and gloried in it and, for all its ills, revere it still. And thus I am able to go on believing in the good that surely must still lie deep in the core of every human heart. And as we strive honorably to meet our destiny, our moment of truth, collective and individual, what better way to await the *déluge*, the poet asks (X.J. Kennedy, I think it was) than to write a poem? I couldn't agree more, for Poetry is my art, my passion. It is my comfort and consolation and my conscience, my delight in the present and the past, and my faith in a divine and earthly future or us all.

Nature, Art, Love, Poetry, Faith, the World...! All of these profound mysteries, and more, are ours to contemplate and draw upon. What more can an artist-poet ask of his Muse? I find, however, in trying to assign my poems into intended niches, any one of the above, that no single poem can limit its subjective essence to one category alone but, inherently, embraces many. Like the human heart in love, one poem cannot hold but one emotion alone, but spills over into the many, *all* of the above, each struggling for preeminence. And in that grand *mêlée* love, in all its many forms and manifestations, is most often paramount.

"Requiem", for example, is ostensibly a poem about childhood's rude awakening to the roll call of the real world, but it also celebrates the child's instinctive love for nature, for the comfort of animal companionship; and, later, from the vantage point of maturity and perspective, the ability to relegate the trauma of disillusionment to a more spiritual acceptance is required; and finally the child within us all finds redemption in attempting to revisit the experience in art, in poetry. *Ergo,* in full circle: World, Faith, Poetry, Love, Art, Nature...!

Preface (Continued)

I hope they, these poems, as composed and here offered, will strike a responsive chord with you, my fellow lovers of art, of beauty and of truth, and of love for all our other selves. Is this not our real challenge today, our most rewarding goal in life and love and art, and, most devoutly to be wished, our destiny as worthy human beings? How else can we repay God for the beauty of this world, for life itself, but by giving of ourselves in the act of creating both life and living art, echoing His own artful masterpiece of creation, mankind and the world—His gift of life to us to whom He has given dominion over this bountiful earth and all our fellow creature inhabitants.

May we prove worthy of His artistic/poetic vision and our own!

—Patricia Anne Kirby Craddock

LOVE LETTERS

We speak of many things
Love, you and I
simple things
deep in meaning
sacred to our world.
Of happiness on earth
and hope of heaven,
of tragedies and triumphs
great and small.
Words, many or few
poetic and profound
but always, always,
like St. Paul's,
of love, of love...

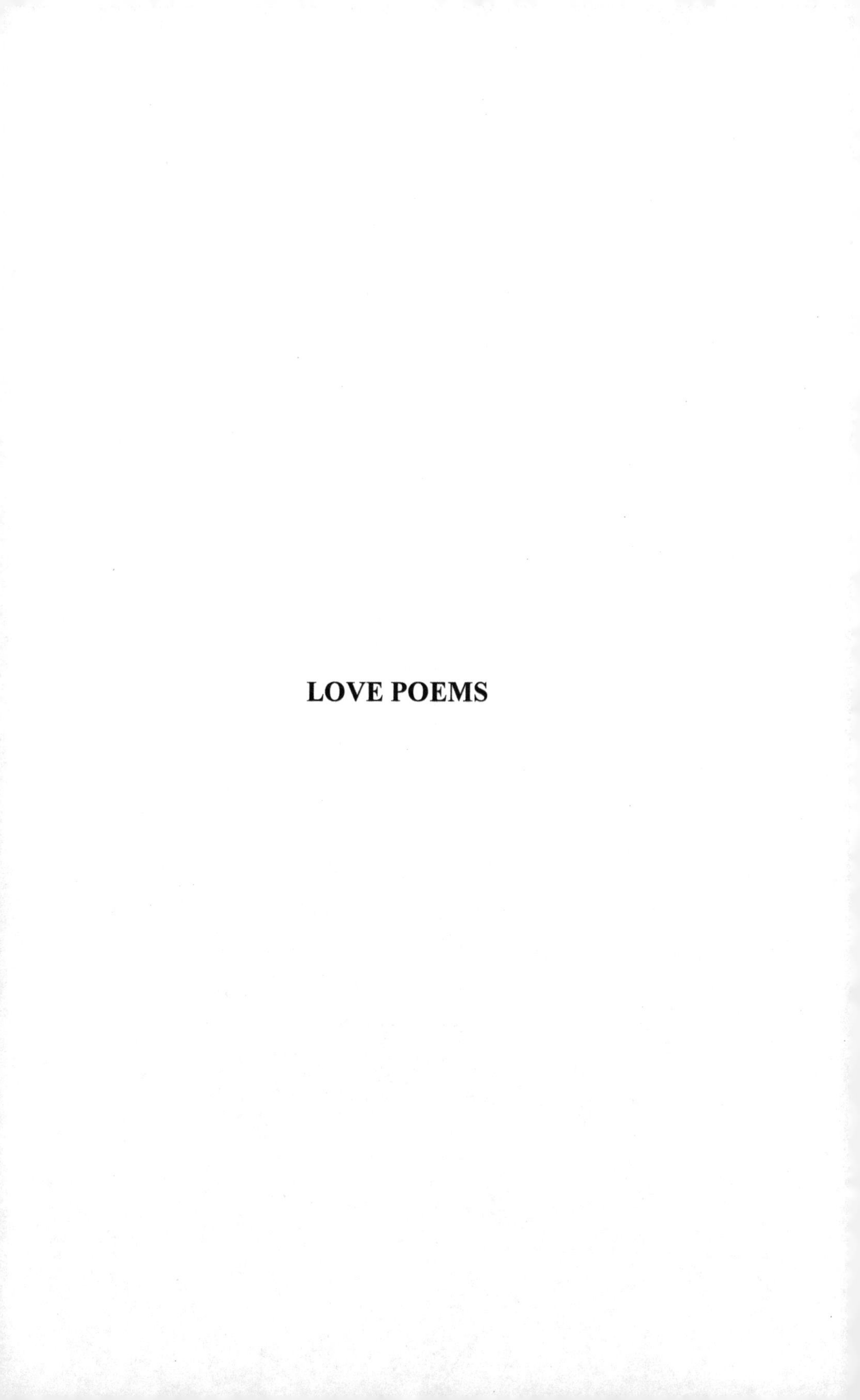

LOVE POEMS

AIDA, TO RHADAMES

O Love, let it be said
we gave our last few breaths
to love...and not in piteous cries
to any man who though he be
Pharaoh himself cannot command
a happier death, or afterlife.

For surely the gods unknown but kind
will not decree that we whose hearts
beat/speak as one shall sleep
together but silent in death forever.
Our pyramid is not of those
dark and dusty temples of kings
entombed in coldness, gold and stone.
More dazzling is our sovereign realm,
and poets weep (and smile!) to hear
praises/hymns to our sacrifice,
treasures now entrusted to
other lovers, other scribes.

And if thieves come, wreaking sacrilege,
or honored men to pay homages,
what will they find in this sacred place
but Aida and her Rhadames,
still wrapped in eloquent embrace,
in words of love long remembered,
warm and brighter than any sun.

AND I AM CLOTHED IN RAIMENT RARE

My closet waits in fancy dress
that I forget to wear;
my cupboard's dusty vintages
might be *vin ordinaire.*
I dress and drink and dine
on quickest, plainest fare,
eager to return
up our poetic stair.
There, *Poetry* (our banquet!) waits
and I, in raiment rare,
with you—for you—am dancing
with ribbons in my hair!

CAN YOU READ POETRY?

Can you read poetry, in me? In my
dreamy, shy, flirtatious look?
Oh then say I'm true, sublime,
profound enough to rhyme
with you.

Is it innocence or guile,
my playful wink, my soulful smile?

I only know it seems
a divine hand places me,
a thousand miles away,
there, where you are
in the open window of your mind,
each day of three thousand days.

Would once have been enough?

Ah yes! Knowing, as we do,
two poets can speak, and scan, cantos
in one shy, half-hidden smile,
in the twinkling of an eye.

ON RECEIVING A THIRD LOVE LETTER

(In As Many Days)

Lap-spread, your last three letters
fill their destiny/fate
to bear and await
our tenderest regard.
I embrace all in one
gladly submissive glance.

Words so rich, so rare
coined in such humble sweetness
starred with such simple joy
fill my eyes with their brightness
parting my lips in wonder:
light—shining round my breasts
shimmering down my thighs,
turning prose into poetry.

So entranced, as if my due
I dream of your next bejeweling,
body no less than heart,
like Danae eagerly willing
clouds/showers of gold,
like Leda, shyly awaiting
her own conquering swan.

FOR YOUR EYES ONLY

When we lie together like this
face-to-face, I can see
through dreamy, half-opened eyes
your eyes, filling with love,
drinking in all of me,
and you smile
because you are happy
and I am happy because…

your mouth upon mine is like fruit
my kisses have ripened for you,
spilling over with kisses for me,
and they are sweeter than nectar
and they make me more giddy than wine…
and the breath of one enters the other
till the joy of it leaves us breathless,
and we are happier still…

for we know though sometimes we show
our love to many another
this bliss no one else can see
but the God in you-and-me.

THE TROUBADOUR

I. THUS ARRAYED, IN YOUR LOVE

Fare thee well, O my chivalrous Knight.
Dieu et mon Droit go with you.

How sweet to be brave, unafraid
like you, my lord, my liege,
to ride forth on the field of honour,
valiantly, boldly to fight
for all you hold sacred and true.
How comely in your bright armour
shield, plumed helmet, and lance
you joust for your lady's favour,
your virtuous vision held fast.
Then haste to the castle in triumph
to the court's ceremonial gaze
as you make obeisance to your king,
till—at last, at last—I embrace you
with my worshipful, welcoming eyes.

They meet yours so chastely, my lord,
so cooly, over your wine,
but belying my innocent look
I tremble inside at your glance,
warm as your jewels on my breast.
For I'm clothed in your royal colours,
your fragrance, your favourite gown,
and my veil can't conceal my smile
as the blossoms entwined in my hair
I place there, like a kiss, on your brow.
Then apart from the curious throng
and safe from my father's view
I rejoice in my heart in secret
as you eagerly, gently unclothe me
with your passionate, ravishing eyes.

Thus arrayed, in your love, I await you.
O my sweet, lovely light of my life.

THE TROUBADOUR
II. CHANSON D'AMOUR ET D'ESPERANCE

Oh pray let me arm you, my lord?

Let me gird you for the great battle
as you mount your horse to ride forth
in search of your Holy Grail...

My arms will entwine around you
my embrace a talisman, charm
against all harm to befall you,
and I'll lay my cheek against yours
and your breast will lie against mine
till nothing can come between us.

I'll wind my veil round your lance
a banner flying on high
that all may know whose heart
you wear like a shield against yours
in lands far away—and then
home to your lady, your love.

I kiss your hand, I implore you
Oh sing me an air as you go!
Oh sing of me fair as you go!
(I kiss your lips and adore you
O my knight, O my troubadour)

Shall I wait for you here in this bower?
Here, where the lemon trees flower,
where the lemon trees fragrantly flower
in your father's peaceful garden?

Oh come back to me soon, belovèd,
back from your brave Crusade.
I shall pray you will be victorious,
then I'll fly to that tower most high
and give thanks for your safe return.

THE TROUBADOUR
III. ELEGY FOR A FALLEN KNIGHT

"Peace, peace! he is not dead, he doth not sleep
He hath awakened from the dream of life..."

- from ADONAIS, by Percy Shelley
(an elegy, upon the death
of his friend John Keats)

Ahimè, this day
seems all too late for all
our dreams of heaven, death
comes all too soon.

Your herald rides in haste bringing news
but from his far-off trumpet call I know
you never again will ride, or sing, to me.

Stunned, struck dumb, too sorrowful to speak
I cover my ears that they not hear
and my eyes that they
may in secret weep.

He, dismounting, distraught, falling
to his knees, cries out his desperate plea:
"Milady—our lord has fallen! He lies
upon the field of battle even now
his life's blood seeps into the earth.
His wounds are mortal oh I fear he dies!
Yet from his pale, cold lips there fell
his warm adieu, his last farewell, to you.

"'tell her,' he murmured, 'tell my lady
if she remember me I will not die.
Say I'll be her Dante still and she
my Beatrice, as I'll still be her Lancelot
and she my Guinevere. On pain of death,'
said he, 'deliver this my last sweet breath
to my lady fair, and this, my faithful kiss.
Tell her I'll wait in Paradise for her,
such rhymes far more sublime for love of her,
and God. Go...give to her my heart,
my fond embrace, these parting words...'"

(continuing)

(begin stanza 6)

O dearest knight, then write
those verses in my heart, sing them
to my soul—my eyes cannot yet see,
so filled are they with weeping.

Soon they'll bring you home upon your shield,
and my veil—your banner—that I may
bind up your grievous wounds,
anoint them with my tears,
giving all that's mortal that I've loved
to heaven, as God's own angels bear
all that is immortal to Our Lord.

Ah, but where but <u>there</u> have we dreamed—
to meet, live, love again, in that sacred place?
You, who are my Francis now,
and I, your Lady Clare.

LINES FROM A POET STILL IN LOVE

with William Shakespeare

"...thank...God for my humility!" (Richard III)

Can one faithful poet still give breath
to life and death and love in such a world's
mockery of the past?

Poetry, art, faith. It's all the same:
unfrock the old, anoint the new. Or so
say the modern gods of art, sacred and profane.
But we endure what whirlwinds reap, and swear
never to bend to fashion's whims, and go on
creating what this world disdains.

Were we born centuries too late?

"We few, we happy few, we band of brothers...." (Henry V)

Always looking back—for so nostalgia views
other idylls, idols, places, times as far
more grace-full rhymes.

I spin out my sonnets full of hope,
like the spider's strong yet tender lines,
into the oppressive air. Hoping,
before the heavens weep, to entwine
one kindred soul. But, alas,
you're no longer there.

"The time is out of joint...." (Hamlet)

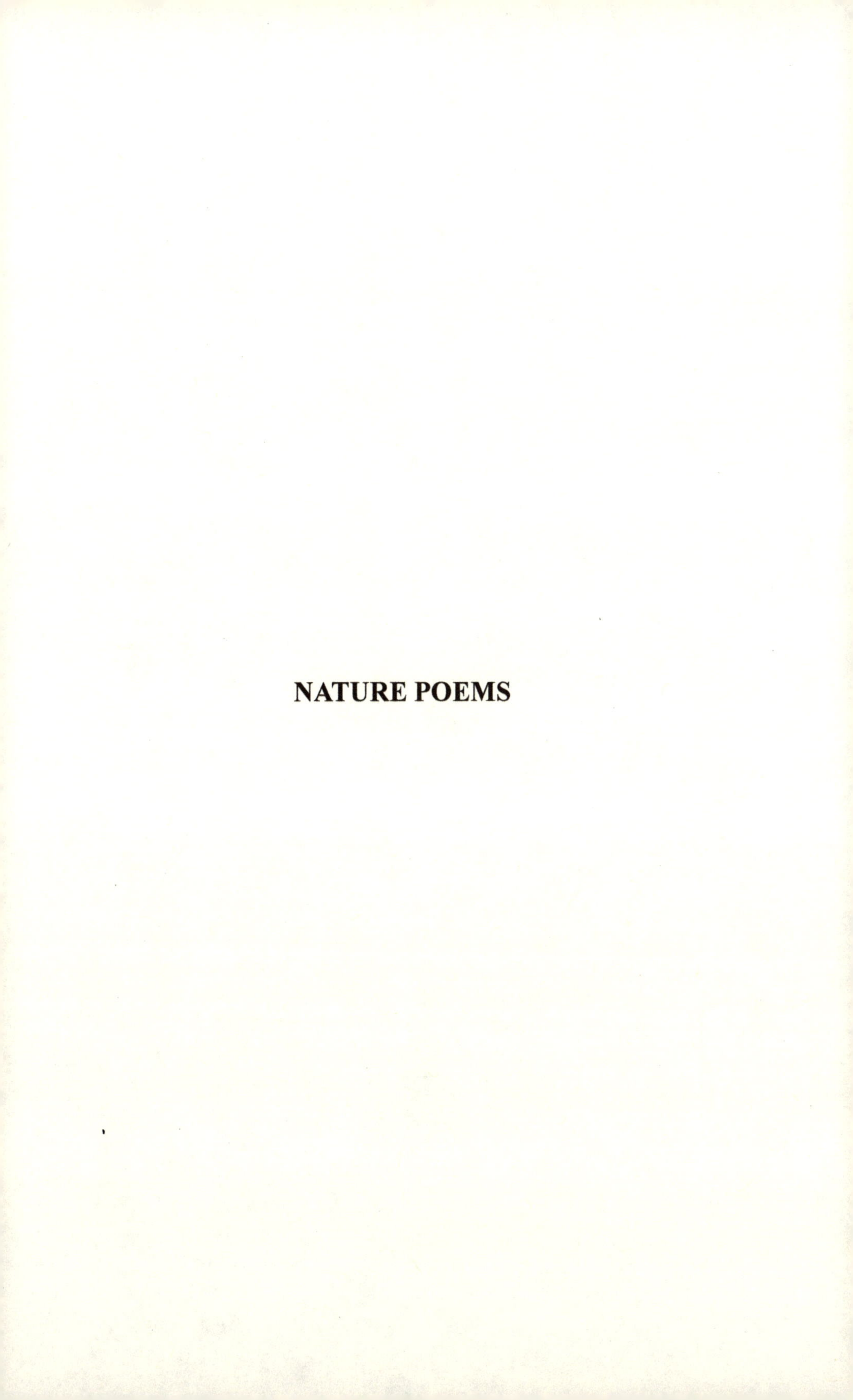

NATURE POEMS

POET LAUREATE OF ANTS

Walking my cat on his leash, at the vacant lot next door
through grasses cool to the skin, in antemeridiem dew,
we pause more often than not, stop more than we start,
as one in our fondness to greet chipmunk, squirrel and bird.
Tethered together we meet one another's need to drowse
in this sunlit summer field of fragrant clover and fern.
Sphinx-like, regally prone, the cat reclines at length,
willing his eye to charm a careless one on the wing.
Conversely, I sink to my knees, my eyes drawn down to earth
to the species there refining their antediluvian arts.
Caterpillar, spider and ant make their appointed rounds,
spared human passions to be other than where they are,
to be other than what they are.

And yet, who can tell? What animates their spirits,
quickens their would-be souls? Man alone aspires,
or so it has been said; only man can write a poem.
But surely they too must pine to triumph at what they do,
to cry out in joy and pain in whichever language they speak
to the infinite God of us all. Do they, too, not yearn
to be poet laureate of ants, to spin a prize-winning web,
to fly, chrysalis-free, in splendor hitherto unseen?
And we, of grandiloquent dreams, who still do believe
in all things seen and unseen, are awed above all to feel
divine creation stir not only in ourselves
but in worlds within worlds
within worlds.

EARTH WATCH

Amid wars and rumors of war, our pastime of self against self,
we try to understand the meaning of it all. From Afghanistan
to Bosnia, Ireland, Zaire…Israel, Iraq, Palestine….

Nature, too, is beyond our control.
Floods cover half the earth, drought over the rest.
Earthquakes, tornadoes, hurricanes, storms….
All the shocks we are heir to, man-made and divine.
Stunned, we can but wondering turn
away from the far to the near
away from the great to the small
away from the many back to one's own
struggle, like Jacob, with God.

* * *

Dripping water and sweat from this pitiless southern sun
I carry drinking pans to a parched field nearby
to succor the birds and the wild things watching,
beaks, mouths agape—too hot to flee, to fly.
My reward? Watching a family of crows with their young
stepping in and out, dipping to drink and bathe.
Seeing my all too human need to play God,
somehow to confer life above death
upon those over whom I am given dominion.

Sometimes, for all our compassion we are overcome
with trying to save the whole world.
We discover that we are not God, after all,
and we do the little we can.

REQUIEM

Walking home from school one day,
age nine or so, an only child
given a benevolent view
of a world well dreamed of, scarcely known,
I came upon a cracker box of wonder:
rude home for three newborn kittens
discarded by some heartless wretch
in a vacant lot. Waiting there, piteous
yet trusting in their innocence
(and ignorance of man), for their mother,
or some samaritan, or savior. Thrilled,
fondling their nuzzling softness,
trying to soothe their mewling cries,
I rushed them home to mine,
As sure as they of her
expected welcome. Eager
as any lonely child for such
long-desired pet companions. They seemed
a gift to me from heaven! But—
take them back—she decreed; and
dumb with disbelief, much
too accustomed to follow orders
even when, as then, unspeakable,
I obeyed.

Useless now to try to find extenuation,
for her, for me, for that other one.
Poverty? Depression? The times?
A poverty of self, of spirit. Untimely
stillborn death of courage and conviction.
Given some later, better time (than 1929)
I know I could have saved them. (continuing)

(begin stanza 3)

How they've haunted me, those poor doomed creatures.
How faintly still I hear their fading cries.
How sadly the veil of innocence
falls from childhood eyes. Pandora's box
could not set free more mixed, quixotic
feelings these long years: distrust
of my own mother for teaching such
indifference to suffering. Self-reproach
for irresoluteness, a little act of charity
passed by. Outrage for that other. And finally
compassion, and forgiveness, for us all.

But it was I who took them back,
back to that barren field, back to their
Gethsemane, Golgotha, their last quiet
resting place. Anointing them with my tears,
promising to remember, to this day.

So in our innocence and ignorance we
perpetuate our inhumanity,
and try to compensate for our long-lost passions,
to mourn life's tragedies, great and small.
Crucifixion; holocaust; war; death—in all its fateful forms.
Trying to elevate even the most prosaic deaths
to something we can bear to contemplate:
to a kind of greatness...to poetry.

SILVIA E IL SATIRO * (for DJL)

Silvia—such idyllic landscape
frames your naturalness of form.
What poem can hope to equal art's
paean to your naked charms?

Such airy vistas through the trees
spill their gleaming light upon you,
nymph reposing, dreamed of/real.
do you spurn or half invite
the satyr yearning to seduce you,
or do you hold your beauty worthy
of love more sacred than profane?

Then has your artist eagerly
lain with you on that grassy knoll,
doubly there immortalizing?

Domenichino, Bolognesse—
protégé of Popes and prelates
Gregory, Aldobrandini
e Farnese *e* Borghese.
Is your landscape near that city
where Dante *e* Petrarca studied,
near the river valley sloping
to the Adriatic sea?

And did your willing spirit yield
to nature's fleshly passions deep,
rising from her freshened streams
to paint such fair and sylvan scenes?

(continuing)

(begin stanza 6)

What poet could not/would not lose
himself between desire and truth
in such pastoral shape and setting,
in your artist-painted phrasings,
in your Silvia's love-struck gaze?

And are the years four hundred since
Dante from those other depths
rose, reborn, to poetry?
And will, three hundred hence, another **
Domenichino drape with praise
his poetic landscaped days?

* ("Silvia and the Satyr"—painting, in the National Gallery at Bologna, Italy, by Domenico Zampieri, called *Domenichino*, Italian painter from Bologna, 1581-1641)

** (Dominick James Lepore, of Enfield, Connecticut and Boston, Massachusetts, USA, the late Italian-American poet and translator, 1911-1990)

POMPEII AND HERCULANEUM—A.D. 79

Cities of the sleeping dead, museums of slumbering flesh and bone
interred in earth's last long embrace—we would not awaken you
from that deep sleep, tomb-quiet spell, otherworldly atmosphere
where never haunted tear nor smothered sigh
shall ever sound again until some other, eternal rendezvous.
Nor would we interrupt your hard-won rest,
your too brief mortal span, your dust-encrusted place
to look upon your once-embodied shapes restored,
preserved in ashen plaster cast, undisturbed in grave and grace.
Master and slave, husband and wife, mother and child and,
faithful to the end, a loyal fallen canine friend.

Two millennia past you lived, loved, toiled, played and prayed
under blue Campanian skies, then-benign Vesuvian hills.
Benevolent Mediterranean gods laid garlands at your feet!
Sea-and-sun-kissed temples, walls, Forums once for living players
hold mute actors now, your curtained stage one day to be unveiled
for impassioned artists/poets to awe-inspire the world
with their timeless truth: life is short, but art endures.

Told by Pliny of that dreadful day—that hot, late August noon-into-night that saw
two thousand beings die—we try not to visualize, or hear, those too sudden overtures
to nature and to fate, yet we *feel* earthquake and volcano raining flames all too real,
thundering lightening-piercing darkness soon consuming that last little day-glow caught
in a pale eclipsed and yellowed orb, the sun... *"sicklied o'er with the pale cast of thought"*.
A thick pall turns stricken air to breathlessness and stumbling footfalls vainly to and fro
as churning waters part from burning shores. Subterranean tremors shock earth and sea,
land and sky tremble, mock hail-stones dance/reach to the highest tree-tops, branch and leaf,
and mud-lava, serpent like, all good omens spent, slinks and slithers, coils and strikes, and
stiffens over all. Then, when the last cries of fear and grief wane, only the echoes of agony
remain—unspeakable even for the amphitheatre; and anguish—unutterable but by the poet,
and yet, beyond all words, and poems, to tell. (continuing)

(begin stanza 4)

But surely your last thoughts returned happily to dwell
on all your deities—Egyptian, Mythic, Pagan...Christian...?
As on this world's divine and earthly joys conceived
within the act and art of love?—*as ours, too, would have been.*
And upon Olympian and Parnassian and Arcadian heights
where faith and intellect collide, and reconcile with love?
And on your Classic sculpted marbles and mosaics,
your painted, frescoed and wall-paneled architecture, art,
born of your joined inheritance—Etruscan, Roman, Greek?
Rest well, then...together, and at peace. Forever intertwined.
Pale as the ash enwereathing you, enshrined in beauty that consoles.
To gaze on such a tender, tragic scene, yet heaven-wrought,
gives birth to human pity in the gods themselves.
And touches our Romantic souls. Facing terror as we do throughout
the night, and arrows that fly by day, we, too, turn back to love of art
and to the art of love—in which most pure and sure recourse on earth
from life's uncertainties resides our certainty of life eternal.
And all our comfort lies in these, and in invoking
a merciful, and real, God of our own.

TSUNAMI

An Elegy for Southeast Asia—26 December 2004.

Now shall we tell our inmost thoughts—of that profound
moment of truth, between breath and death? We, too, with you,
are borne on that cresting wave, that wall of wild sea water breaking
away from Earth's great core: that quaking mating-marriage bed
of thrusting plate and yielding crust, spawning cosmic birth.
Yet who can think and speak, rejoice and weep like Deity,
in such divinely-rhymed superlatives of anguish and of joy!
Although, God knows, we've seen His Magnitude, His sovereignty, before.
But has Earth itself ever thus trembled on its course, its plane,
its axis, fixed, ordained—and long held to be—steadfast?
Once death and I nearly met on fate's threshold of near-drowning,
in a mere three feet of careless seas—undertow, I suppose,
on such a bright and carefree day. On familiar Southern shores
edging the Atlantic. Upended, swallowing from that shallow brink
of an ocean fathomless, panicked burning throat and eyes cannot tell
if air still somehow waits—or if salvation, somewhere, dwells.
Although soon set aright by a savior, a samaritan nearby.
Did you reach out in mute appeal for fragile human touch,
floating on tides of hope and dread, those rising falling ocean swells?
As brother, sister, parent or mate, husband, wife, lover or child
held fast to your saving grasp—or cried out "Farewell!" Thousands
perished so, and yet the wonder is the miracle that graces souls
to survive, and rise, whether the body lives or dies.
It's said some primal urge and scheme, some inner sense God-given
from Creation's time, enables animals to circumvent upheaval
by such planetary tolls, earthquake or tidal wave, and seek
the hills above, that place where safety lies. So might we,
in all our sudden unforeseen earthly agonies of shock and aftershock,
embrace alike our days of utter joy, our nights of bitter grief, keeping fixed
our gaze, our thoughts and dreams, our hopes and fears, on higher ground.

EXILE

Forty days and more the earth
has lain helpless, heartlands
prostrate under the rule
of cruel, merciless drought,
her creatures once carefree
fleeing in desperate thirst
for life-giving rain.

The African plain lies parched;
seared, that once lush home
to antelope...wildebeest... Hear
the unearthly quiet?

The last water hole has been sucked dry,
its mud caked hard, cleaved to the sun-
baked savannah, like fevered tongues
stuck to the roofs of mouths
of pitiful lumbering herds
dumbly, wonderingly seeking
mercy of nature and God.

Still, the thundering hooves fall
silent with night, fitfully sleeping.
(dreaming of longed-for return?)

Poor beasts. They know they must roam
far from there: must rise with the cool
circling moon and depart, leave the deep,
green-fringed bush, find water and hope before
another sun-scorched day. But where?
Doomed, too soon to be brought to earth,
too proud to show it, they struggle on.

THE CAGED LIONESS

Cornered, she lies in a corner of her cage,
too exhausted to pace. Her beauty is queenly
still, her presence regal, though she is prisoner
not only of her cage, in this pale
zoological Eden, but of body and mind.

What does she see as she reclines there,
distantly watching? What companions
of freedom and youth pad silently
through brain and heart? Does she recall
pacing the grassy savannah, tawny coat mottled
by sun and cloud? Stalking prey for her mate,
of all beasts, king? Giving birth, suckling
her cubs, on the open plain? For she had no fear,
no predator, but man. Man who was given dominion
over her, who sought to contain her wild magnificence,
who thought to save her, and gave her refuge.

For a time then, she paced, lunged
crashing against her bars, wounding herself
and those of us watching, dying to be
free to be wild, her rumbling coughs and cries
answering the call of the moon and the night.

Now she awaits her fate: to die in captivity.
But her benevolent Creator has made her
last years placid, accepting, knowing
her days are but few. And there's nobility
in her vigil. Soon the fierce light
in her once commanding gaze will go out.
the wavering flame of her life will extinguish
and she will go forth to her lord and master,
to lie down with lambs again, in Paradise.

(written for my mother, at 94, bedridden and restrained, in her last illness)

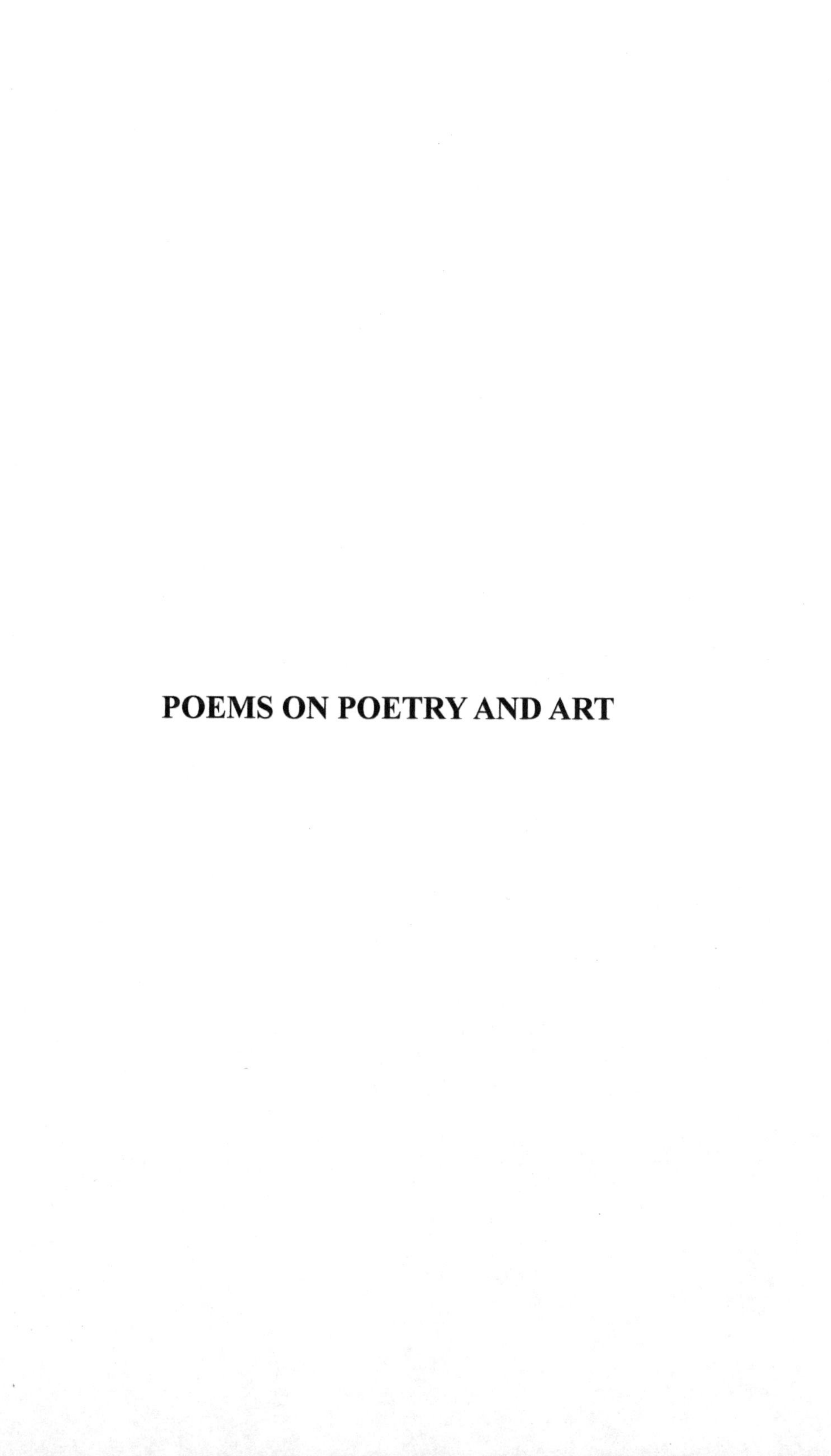

POEMS ON POETRY AND ART

GENIUS

"Madame Bovary, c'est moi!"
(Gustave Flaubert, of his novel)

Through but a chosen few God claims His right
to speak—in music, art, and poetry.
to teach, that by example we may see
the grace of genius striving for the light.

In simplest eloquence, from sage to youth
what greater legacy can they impart
than translating visions, from the soul, the heart,
into plainest, universal truth?

How do they teach? They write, paint, carve, compose.
Creating, as things are or as they seem;
unfearing death, knowing art cannot die.
Oh to be such a one, blessed as those
God smiles upon! Dreaming peerless dreams,
gazing—on one's own art—to cry: *There*…am I.

ON A BUS RIDE TO SOMEWHERE

(Modern Art, and Verse)

Some of us see you
boarding the bus
in your whimsical fashion,
erratically garbed in a mix-match of clothing,
muttering gibberish,
eccentric, disturbing.

Some of us
cannot see you at all.

Such a nice day,
says the elderly lady
obliviously clutching
affluence, securely,
in shopping-bag-filled
reassuring remoteness.

I view you confused,
enigmatic, pathetic
yet purposeful somehow
to someone all-knowing
just where you are going
in your own meandering
seemingly random,
(would-be romantic?)
artistic/poetic way.

CARVINGS

What lies beneath the pure baptismal veil
of uncarved marble? Does the sculptor know,
divine, like Michelangelo,
his stirring figures' cries as they bewail
their captive plight, beyond the pale
of our finite sight? But poets, too, bestow
upon their eager page, lines, row on row,
dazzling as Carrara stone, or any grail.

And poets still unknown, unsure, unsung
share in common something fair, and great:
travail, from which all art is wrung
against all odds, in hope, or fate.
So with marble, flesh, and poet's tongue,
Gods and men labor to create.

THE GREAT BUDDHAS OF BAMIYAN

Silent and still a thousand years
you've stood and gazed as history passed,
surveying centuries beyond
the cannon-fire of Genghis Khan.
Buddhist and Muslim, sacrosanct.
Now you tremble, doomed to fall
to a modern-day barbarian,
new-age iconoclast: your own
gun-and-self fragmenting hand,
O Afghanistan.

So Savonarola, faith gone awry,
dared to preach and immolate
great art and poetry. To such a one
art signifies a calumny: idolatry.
Now, shadows fall from a darker age
and echoes rise—like the hollow changing
of a bent and empty vessel
at the bottom of a desert well gone dry.
Sounding a solemn death knell,
a sad farewell, lamenting human cries
above the deafening silencing
of sanity and reason;
if not, quite yet,
of civilization.

ON DANTE And His Language

"Dante and Shakespeare", they say, "divide the world between them;
        There is no third."
Ah, Dante, Dante! how fairly you uphold this equal truth—
you, whose life and art are measured out in thirds:

Lingua più bella del mondo

The Trinity, your Holy rule—Father, Son and Spirit;
Beatrice, purest dream—thrice blessed unto your path;
three goads along your mortal way—outrage, exile, zeal;
triple visions—Hell, Purgatory, Paradise—on your immortal climb;
the tercets of your epic verse, in peerless *terza* rime.

Lingua Toscana, lingua di Dio

So finely wrought is Heaven's grace
into its earthly counterpart, the city-state
and country of your birth:
Florence, Tuscany, Italy…Dante Alighieri,
that by the exaltation of your lusty mother tongue
your *Comedy* has matched it to its noble parent, Latin,
and by your passion spent to heal our self-won scars
you have shown us, too, how to win the stars.

FRAGMENT PRESERVED IN AMBER

Once, I think I saw some glowing fossil
perfect of its kind
preserved in amber,
all its tranquil beauty timeless sealed
unvanishing, unvanquished
aeons past:
once part of creation's gift—a spider—
just a little thing but such a triumph
of design, elegant, and pure of line;
stilled, in all its earthly grace and grandeur,
like doomed Pompeii's dust-encrusted flight,
until at last revealed
to some explorer's random view,
unknown, unknowingly
but reverent.

I think, now, some other excavator
in future search for worthy artifacts,
if not for what *we* knew as life, and art,
may stumble on such fragment of a poem
aeons hence
in faded, cryptic script
yet with its rhyme once perfect, plain
to its creator still,
and to that one created for,
by their amber light;
so spared from Alexandria's tragic fate
and, though a splendor barely understood
by its late discoverer,
regarded humbly,
with respect.

IN COMPETITION WITH SHAKESPEARE

"Shakespeare and Dante", they say, "divide the world
between them; there is no third."
(Dante—from heaven and hell…
Shakespeare from teeming earth)
So you, O gifted Bard, bequeath this fair-shared truth
from your storied "sceptered Isle".

And we: today's impassioned scribes—how do we see you now?
How do we view your art, from this world's point of view?

You are the sovereign sun
no armor can prevail,
You are our ruling star
no arrow can impale.
You, unmeasured mountain,
we scale because you're there,
as you, unfathomed sea,
we sail we know not where.

You are the land we seek
beyond the ocean's roar;
we pit our craft against you,
straining for the shore.
You, unwearied moon,
still light our fainting heart,
and so, O Poet's god,
you make—or break—our art.

(continuing)

(begin stanza 5)

In sum you are the soul of our ambition
but not the depth and width and height of self,
for in our reach towards excellence as yours,
your poet's/playwright's proud, prolific pen,
who else is there to grasp your truthful precept
of faithfulness to self—except ourselves?

Yet if we speak the truth true are requires,
and sweat the costly blood our fame demands,
is it not God who laurel-wreathes our brow
with glad resolve worthily to compete,
immortalizing man as well as art?

Thus, if we cannot touch you it shall not dim our aim
(O Unobtainable we would attain!)
To prove to you our meriting, Shakespeare—
no less than to our other idol, Dante—
our destiny: to seal our trinity.

IN REMEMBRANCE OF SIDNEY LANIER

Long you have shone, Lanier
shining still warmly upon us
as the sun's infinite radiance
illumines our longing for truth.
Your voice
in its music
lingers
past the woods
through the glades
beyond death;
a song of things known
and unknown.
And the soft coastal winds
in the marsh
fill the poet
as the poem
with life's breath.

Consumed in your passion to live
evangel of lyric, of love
to speak of the ultimate dream
not to die with the dream unuttered
transcending your burning struggle
you reconcile nature with God.

Bright scholar
brief beacon of light
your poetry speaks to us all
that *feeling*
is all to the artist
and still can be all to man.

(continuing)

(begin stanza 4)

Your spirit your words
are mirrored
not in sand
not even upon
your beloved mysterious islands
your mystical marshes of Glynn
but tenderly bravely
undying
in the minds
and hearts
of men.

ON POETRY AS ART

To begin a poem is to bare the heart
to all the passions one is heir to
for beauty and for truth.

From such vast array of art, present and past,
the poet, like the artist, trembling with a lover's
eager eye and touch, moves ardently to ponder
which brush to use, which canvas, which rich colors'
bold and subtle shadings, to seduce the Muse.
That same sleeping waking fever seizes
the poet's brain for he, too, paints—with words.
And as the artist paints over his mistakes,
the poet, when his *mot juste* dances out of sight,
can uproot and right the wrong, taking time to savor
meaning's fine nuance, reveling in art's paradox
like those of life and love: its pleasures and its pain.

Where than to begin invoking inspiration?
In Poetry? Art? Love? Nature? Faith? The World?
What does the mind's eye seek before giving birth
to epic-lyric stanzas-cantos, rhymed or free
lines the world one day, remembering, may speak?
What idylls lie waiting to be given to the light
in verses bearing one aspiring poet's fate?
Philosophies undreamt of?—in heaven, and on earth?

Influences jostle, crowd the varied stages
of our common aspirations. Whose voice,
whose siren call shall we listen to, and hear?
God's own, through art, to Michelangelo?

(continuing)

(cont. stanza 4)

Dante's poems of love to *Beatrice* ? Faust's
jousts with Mephistopheles—still *"going to and fro"*?
Shakespeare's royal speeches? Shelley's skylark singing
"profuse strains of unpremeditated art"? Or Blake's (and our)
requiem and lament: *"Tyger Tyger* (yet) *burning bright /*
in the (threatened) *forests of the night"*?

Custodians of poetry that is real,
guardians of laurels yet to win,
like or nay, past our modern ways
with brush and pen, thought and word we are
bound to honor those who strove before us.
But all our jaded imitations, pale, heart-wringing,
all our hard-wrought innovatings, must serve us well
or not at all. Change for the sake of change
is as sterile, as abortive, as art that languishes stillborn.
Still, we have the will to fashion, for poetry as art,
some fertile, fruitful mating-ground unthreatened
by homage to the future or the past. For all our famed
artistic and poetic craft we're still ambivalent—human
to the end—both subject to our passion to hold on
to life, to earth, to those who, too, once struggled for the light,
and to reach for heaven, beyond Dante's stars—to begin anew, to *write*
poetry the world will long acclaim, for love, for art.

(*N.B.* Line 28's *"Beatrice"* may be read as in the Italian)

GRAY SATURDAY AT OGLETHORPE

(Alone in the Great Hall)

The world
steeped in gray
sky, landscape, stone—
as I am clothed in grayness,
draped in somber mood.

Encumbered only by silence
thunderous and still
these ancient walls,
Oxford hued and hewn,
peaceful lie.

Still, in company with ages,
we move—the earth and I—
toward enlightenment,
Approaching (light years away)
the sun, the center of brightness.

EGYPT, THE ETERNAL

Eyes upon Sphinx and Pyramids
veiled in mystery through time
beneath Egyptian sun and sand—
awed, before such vast graves
immortalizing finite man,
Pharaoh and slave,
we stand.

On the Giza Plateau these tombs endure
four thousand years, four millennia,
since Cheops decreed his Great Pyramid:
one hundred thousand slaves to raise
two million two-ton stones to face
the four cardinal points of the universe.

In Cairo of sixteen million souls
in Egypt's Museum repose the gold
burial mask and Royal Mummy
mirroring vain earthly pomp
and panoply—the reign of one
young dead king, Tut-Ankh-Amun.

Nearby, a Royal Scribe awaits,
his eyes of quartzite and obsidian,
eyelids, green malachite and copper.
What do they see?—serenely gazing
on splendors of such worldly glory,
on mysteries still scarcely known.

Perhaps they look now only inward—
as other scribes are wont to do—
content to tell the world of those
ancient wonders they have seen,
reflecting what such marvels mean
in glorious poetry and prose.

DAUGHTERS OF THE RHINE AT PLAY *

"Wie scheint im Schimmer ihr hell und schon!" **
("How you shine in the glimmering light, so bright and fair!)

So fair it gleams, your alabaster
flesh against that turquoise sea,
upon those emerald waves, caressing
your glowing breasts, gold-flowing hair.
Such shimmering beauty casts its own
light upon those secret ways
deep within the river Rhine
from your hidden guarding place
to the sun-lit gold you hold
high over rock and river bed.
Lure and allure for Alberich! —
that thief who'd steal you both away:
the gold to forge a magic ring,
yourselves to sing and play.

Now Art's lush impasto weds
Music's bold iconoclast
whose first crescendo-notes evoke
the river's rhythmic, rushing course.

O Daughters of the Rhine, sublime
in your immortal loveliness,
star-crossed, spellbound, in sound and sight,
by *Rheingold's* glorious *leitmotiv*,
we know that we could never claim
that ring to rule the world as gods
nor ever swear, thereby,
to give up Love.

* From the painting of that name by German artist Hermann Hendrich, 1893 (in the poet's collection)

** From the libretto of Richard Wagner's opera *Das Rheingold* (1853-4), Scene I (Alberich to the Rhine Maidens).

FOR MY FAMILY AND FRIENDS NURTURED ON POEMS

For all the times I've sat writing
poems instead of preparing
gourmet meals for you,
for all my clumsy attempts
at cooking and keeping house,
for all the domestic talents
I might have mastered
and didn't...forgive me?

Do not remember, I implore,
the pedestrian foods I served,
the books and papers and magazines
piled ceiling-high everywhere,
the dust collecting, beds unmade,
while I hurried through
what I had to do,
to return to Poetry!

Remember instead that
I loved to shop, spending energy,
time, on family, friends,
that I always had time for pets,
for birds and chipmunks and dogs
and cats (and fish and frogs!),
time to listen and give advice:
"The Lord will provide", "this, too,
shall pass", and "Peace..."
and "Love one another..."

(continuing)

(begin stanza 4)

Remember to laugh as we laughed together,
to hug and kiss one another,
to take time to walk with a child,
to inspect a bug, collect a rock,
to swing and play and read a book.

Remember to seek the consolation
and comfort of God, each day while you can.
Remember we live not by bread alone
but by music and dance, language and art,
by God's Word and all we utter
to tell Him and each other
"I shall love you...forever."

Remember that dreamers and mystics and poets
have food to eat others know not of...

TO LISA

(Leonardo, before his painting of Mona Lisa)

Madonna, toscana, Lisa. Dear God!
What rapture have we captured in your face?
All I revered in woman: is it odd

that my own dreamed-of mother bears the trace
of your beauty? And heaven's royal Queen.
To honor *her*, all talents must abase

their struggle toward perfection's fairest mean.
But if you are not perfect, nor am I,
although within your countenance serene

I glimpse those selves which, with me, seem to die:
child, wife, lover, friend. Banners high unfurled
could not tell me more; genius cannot lie.

Like Dante's Beatrice, angel-lips curled
in enigmatic smile convey *the world!*

THE LAST CANTO

What anguish in the dying of a poet.

The waning strength, the still and ever faithful
ardor of the soul. Whether
to try—to go on creating, or lay by
art's seeming faithless, unrequiting love
and seek some late flowering of hope,
some long past due acclaim.

Fear and passion, his love affair with words,
beat, with his very blood, ageless in his veins.
He knows Keats' grief for verses yet unwritten,
Poe's deepest dreams of poetry to be,
and walks with Dante through that wood
so dark, so arduous, and drear.

Perhaps he will begin his final canto.

Or lay down his pen, his rhymes, his figured lines.
His poem-play's the thing: to give it birth
he would follow Dante on that climb
through all the earth. And dare compete
with Shakespeare, exalting royal kings.

Will it pass the test, be brought to the light,
or languish—in some poor, obscure, archival tomb
with the rest? With all those poems aborted, lost
to false and fickle gods of fame and success.

Do not die disheartened, Poet. Art, too, may rise.

Of such empyreal gifts—had the Creator rested
too soon that formless night before
His first dawning day to be—
would we have been deprived.
The sun...the moon...the stars.
Filling poets' eyes and so
the world, with dazzling poetry.
The turning, and the meaning,
of darkness into Light.

THE LAYERED GRAVES OF BABYLON (Archaeology, to Antiquity)

And where are your certain charms of old...your constancies of Art ?

Where are they now? Those ruins and remnants past compare
of Nimrod and Ninevah...Ur and Uruk.... Those relics and remains
of ruling kingdoms, ancient empires, once striving/thriving tribes—
Sumerian-Babylonian-Akkadian-Assyrian—You, our forebears,
whose palaces and ziggurats, towers and temples and tombs,
cylinder seals and tablets, cuneiform codes of law comprised
our heritage from humanity: our gifts of poetry and art
from you who paid tribute, incised in gold and stone and clay,
to cities, kings, and deities. And common human scribes.

There, Civilization bloomed, flowered, flourished
through panoplies of time, layering man on man.
And now, how can we endure, bear to look upon
this spectacle of Baghdad's sack, deflowering
of a fruitful realm, this ravishing of the history
of modern-day, and ages-old, Iraq?

Add to war's base tragedies of man's lost lives: his imperiled Art.
Of all the artistic/architectural antiquities feared lost
from that prolific earth, that yet pregnant land,
may there be others waiting still on that vast plain
within that fertile crescent valley there
between the Tigris and its twin, Euphrates;
biding time *in situ*, in Civilization's cradle—
that empire-city-riverbed, that rich pre-natal cord,
that thread entwining history's birth, linking humankind.

(continuing)

(begin stanza 5)

So many have been born and died, whirled into maelstroms of wars and time.
So much has crumbled into the dust of civilizations once artful and alive.
Or given leave for safekeeping to custodians, curators,
galleries and museums—and amateur acquisitive collectors.
Think of the plundered Parthenon: those classic Attic trusts,
the Elgin marbles. Of Egyptian pharaohs, grave-robbed of *entree*
to their eternal afterworld. And all the Mesopotamian marvels
raped, taken, bought and sold like conquered living flesh
bound forever out of context for the art/slave markets of the world.

O finite man, O fragile art! Remembering is but to weep.

And you, looter, vandal, thief: will you restore your unearned trophies
to their rightful provenance—or hold on for ransom against yet another
war-torn time? Deface, destroy, melt down for precious ore?
Or simply sell—for bread...or oil?

Silver harp and golden bull, copper head and ivory plaque...
Sculpture, statue, bowl and lyre...Mosaic, marble bust, and vase
carved of alabaster...Stone relief, stela, slab...Jewels of gold
and precious gems, once adorning sovereign queens. *Our most poetic*
treasure trove: wingèd lion, mythic god, heroic man, long-crownèd king.
Shall we ever see your figured like again—ever hear you speak,
your long-buried secrets told? Come, let us seek wise counsel, you and I,
of Babylon's enlightened King. O Hammurabi....

Oh the irony, agony of heart, that we have saved so few
books and manuscripts, tomes and poems and volumes rare
from those whose gift it was to fashion language, our spoken/written art.

(continuing)

(begin stanza 10)

Still, not ours alone to despair, lament, sing elegies too soon to Antiquity
for our grave loss—our cultural patrimony, our desecrated ways,
our once-regnant landscapes laid waste. Surely one day soon
the lions of the desert will roar, and reign, again. *Even you, Alexander,*
breaching Babylonian gates, must feel Rome's warm eager breath
close upon your chariot wheels—a pall upon your ruling star
as you ride triumphant through that city-state. Soon, soon, in time, to learn
great empires build upon great empires, even as they fall.

From unexcavated mounds and sites, from yet unpublished finds,
Archaeology's threatened digs will still yield wonders for our minds
and eyes to feast upon—new and tantalizing glimpses of peoples and
their visions, arts essayed and mastered millennia ago,
even as we welcome back men and artifacts thought lost,
broken or intact. When under amnesty returned,
regained, must we not then swear to take care
of both lives and legacies, refusing to succumb
to our lust for war, our siren song, once more?

And what of Poetry...our other otherworldly art?

Of Torah, Bible and Qur'an—our sung and written Word
of Solomon and shepherd, of prophet, psalmist, seer.
What will be the modern fate of Poetry as art?

Where, indeed, are all our poems commended to the wings of chance?
Dancing in mid-air, daring Dante's stars, far above the rest?
Fragile as birds and struggling wildflowers
delicate but strong, their yearnings, too, aspiring
yet to prove their worth. Are they but ashes now long-interred
though burning still to return, these our bequests,
to a world to which they, too, are loath to say farewell,
even in these inauspicious times for art and rhyme? (continuing)

(begin stanza 15)

Will they be lost forever or yet be unearthed?
Shall we inscribe them once again, on ancient palimpsests,
our paeans to immortality, our *objets d'art* in words?

Will some faithful literary archaeologist-archivist
peruse those words obscure, and excavating find
new treasures to bring forth, to give unto the light?
New works to claim their destiny, human or Divine,
within the covers of a book—opening as though
through museum doors, royal tombs, ancient city gates,
upon a world ever awed by man's monumental
stepping stones and building blocks of poetry and art.

And when some artist-poet, scarcely known, lies dying,
as must all artists, poets, known, unknown, however
death-defying—from war or plague or our all-too-brief
span of appointed time—all men across the centuries returning
to that dust in which eternally commingle
both God-formed bones and man-made mysteries,
splendors all to cry out to ages yet to come, one may still pray
the body of that work that completes the sum
of even one creative life, *oeuvre* if not *chef-d'oeuvre*, bespeaking
the summit of all our aspirations and talents to convey,
may preserve in words, or stone, or clay—
the artist-poet's passion...the soldier's sacrifice...
the believer's creed...the dreamer's dying dream:
to leave a living legend for all time.

(continuing)

(begin stanza 18)

Then, may those wonders hidden, those would-be-epic lines,
those shards of memory and desire, from our war-fragmented times,
stir and fly—mosaic-like—together, and be made whole
for creator and conservator alike; and may it be given
to some brave and dedicated restorer in the field
to resurrect and enthrone in edifices of regard
all that still remains of lives, and art,
once lived well, once well loved.

*

And after our last battle is fought may we, enemies no longer, lie
together, amid our hard-won certainties of beauty and of truth,
among our sacred images, our common human touch embracing
patriarch and progeny alike, peaceful, breast to breast, at rest.

WAR POEMS AND THE WORLD

SUNDAY AFTERNOON, December 7, 1941

(Sunshine Beach, St. Petersburg, Florida)

Tsunami-like, these waters have raced
over half a world to lap and taste
this temptingly vulnerable southern shore.
Dazzled, long drenched in the beauty of each,
as by their playful, graceful spray,
I am lordly, profligate, turning my back
to the changeless, inviolable sand and sea.

My hand, grown weary
with the tossing of bread
to subservient gulls
wheeling and flapping
flatteringly toward me
from miles down the beach,
teases the radio dial, today,
trying to tempt it to say something
newer, somewhat more exciting
than this ancient day's coming Good News,
or the far less promising news of the day.

"We interrupt this program",
(your thoughts, lives...
dreaming, desiring...)
the ethereal voice agonizes,
"to tell you we are at war..."

(continuing)

(begin stanza 4)

The unalterable word assaults my senses,
crawls in my ear like the poison it is—
dispatcher of kings and subjects and princes.
But I cannot bring myself to hate
the destroyer of my kingship, my kingdom,
but, rather, mourn the death of those beaches
already, and destined to be, violated.
Even now, the approaching, encroaching tides
claim these proffered shores, voluptuously waiting.
I gather my remnants of hope of pretending
that nothing has changed, and turn back
to the comfort of unending sameness,
the false consolation of not-quite-yet-knowing,
the growing feeling of no place to hide.

Reproving, remote, the gulls move oceanward,
sensing somehow I have lost control
of my role of benevolent power, protection
over beaches and creatures here and abroad—
those private recesses, sun-spangled reaches
whose sacrosanct beauty already is being
cruelly, violently desecrated.

THE EYE OF MY MIND

(*vers libre*: a song of freedom)

(Dedicated to
Count Leo Tolstoy
(1828-1910)
who, born to the Aristocracy,
wept for the Peasantry)

This quiet night, this tranquil time
between wakefulness and sleep,
caught by that occasional demon of darkness
that sometimes seizes the irresolute spirit of man,
I'm struck by a sudden unbidden conviction
that—although at any moment I may rise
to the challenge of pursuing forgetful sleep—
perhaps in calm outward acceptance or welcome
of this lost art of day-dreaming by day or by night,
or, one might say, of thinking before doing
(as a precept of order, of course, not a denial
of righteous inner passions crying *action*),
survival lies. Suddenly, remembering, I know
what it is to be, and I become, a citizen of the world...

A martyred Jew, from any/every nation,
uninvited guest of unforgivable dishonor,
my honor in (temporary) bondage
to those who have no honor
(whom I shall yet forgive)
at Auschwitz, Treblinka, Dachau;

and the Gulag—

A would-be émigré from Mother Russia,
screaming soundlessly for a pencil stub,
a scrap of paper, a sliver of soap
to *write*, to give to the light,
stillborn if not aborted altogether,
mine and the world's truest poem.

(continuing)

Denied, in our separate human agonies, (begin stanza 4)
our common, essential human rights
to more than food, clothing, shelter—
to life itself, to something once called happiness,
also known in better times as freedom,
and peace (*shalom*, my brother, *shalom!*),
still we possess a certain idealistic (if not naive!)
belief in the good that surely still must lie,
buried perchance, deep in the heart of every man.
To believe so, at least, enables me to rise
above my own death when it comes
and humanity itself to survive.

But is not this our happy secret, our secret strength,
so foreign to the oppressors of the world?
This individual yet universal will endure
the ultimate degradation and ultimately death,
and still to protect, nurture and cherish the *soul*—
the center of our being we call *God*—
knowing there is indeed that part of us made
in likeness of Him incorruptible, which
although thye exterminate us they can never extinguish:
that Love that burns within us like a flame.

In this last human stronghold of spiritual sanctuary—
the inviolable, sacrosanct self—I shall remember always
the joyful pleasures of strolling, un-denied,
the actual and intellectual avenues of the outside world.
Shall they ever know the joy of walking at will inside
the corridors of the mind? Or understand that the self
still may choose its own escape route—the mind's avenues?
Or comprehend the treasures I see (the friends whom I meet)
still gracing the walls of the eye of my mind?
(on the gay boulevards of the eye of my mind) (continuing)

(begin stanza 7)

And even: that royal exile and deposed heir, the Tsar,
weeping for more than my lost throne—for my people,
for all those victims, known or not to me, of my reign,
and for my land in death-and-birth pangs to which I,
and my son's sons, may never return. *(Russia!—*
O my Russia! Must I then live without thee?)

All these and more, across the centuries and globe,
are ravished in the flesh—but not the soul.
All, all with no human refuge to hide
and no place to go but the mind.

Denied, in our separate human agonies,
our common, essential human rights
to more than food, clothing, shelter—
to life itself to something once called happiness,
also known in better times as freedom,
and peace (*shalom*, my brother, *shalom!*)
still we possess a certain idealistic (if not naive!)
belief in the good that surely still must lie,
buried perchance, deep in the heart of every man.

ODYSSEY

In Bosnia-Herzegovina,
a mother ceaselessly searches
for the corpse of her young son.

Barely eleven he wandered
past Serbian lines nine months ago
to be savagely beaten, slain,
never to come home again.

<u>She</u> looks to be a thousand.
Pale, unkempt eyes wild
blazing, burning with grief.

She is mad they say she spits
on Muslim refugees.
To her they must all bear guilt
for the murder of her son.

How does she know? This
her informant once neighbor
now no longer friend
but Muslim enemy claims
to know where the child's body lies.

Taunted, goaded, harassed
by this woman strung out on hate
he eyes here warily.
Crazed, tormented, driven,
this mother who cannot rest

(continuing)

(cont. stanza 6)

until she bids farewell
to her piteous hostage to war,
of her spurned gift to the world,
until she presses a kiss
upon his innocent brow.

Flayed by her tongue, her gaze
her guide fears, yet hopes.
Will she spare him if he prevails,
or kill him, for spite, if he fails?

Eventually they find a fresh grave.
Wailing, cursing, she prays.
On her knees with her hands she unearths
the pitiful wasted remains—a young girl
who sleeps there forever bearing
her trophies of unearned pain.

Sinking deeper in madness
mother and guide wander on,
chained together by hope
in their endless odyssey
through war's hopelessness.

GÖTTERDÄMMERUNG

They are burning books again. In Bosnia-
Herzegovina. Penultimate insult
to civilization—the ultimate being,
of course, war itself, civil or otherwise,
pitting man against himself
on the battlefield of his mind.

They are burning books again, not
for ideology but warmth. Winter is harsh
in Sarajevo. And yet, what warmth
can a thought provide,
the creation of art send forth,
formulation of reason yield?
Little, perhaps—in this unreal, unfair
"real" world—but in our remembered world of ideas...
Ah! *There*, passions ignite, burn hot, inflame minds,
make rhymes to encircle radiant suns.

Oh cry out, take time to remember the ancients:
that torch-lit twilight of the gods of fire and war.
Rome burning for days. Alexandria's libraries
in flames, her archives laid waste. Firenze's
bonfires of books. Then, mourn, too, for the moderns—
Pearl Harbor to Berlin—via Auschwitz, Treblinka, Dachau.
Afghanistan and Iraq; Israel and Palestine. And Russia—
O imponderable one, in your unspeakable intellectual toll
of artistic-literary-philosophic pain.
All, all holocausts, great or small. And then
the ghostly footfalls on Diaspora's bitter plain.

Oh, we are the masters of war alright.
Masters of setting fires,
if not of putting them out.
Wiping his eyes, one writer/reader/lover of books
sighs: To think that I, I who love them so

(continuing)

(cont. stanza 4)

must burn my own books. Reverently
laying another on his sacramental fire—
like Abraham's altar to offer up Isaac,
like Rodolfo burning his poems to stay warm—
weeping, this lover of words consigns
his offspring of his mind,
his brainchild of the self,
his labor of love,
his life's blood, his manuscripts,
to the Phoenix-arising flames.

Is it a consolation—an absolution—
that he does this only to keep
body and soul intact? Maybe
the loveliest things are meant to be
ephemeral, passing, sweet.
And the only way to hold on to gifts
as immortal/eternal as life,
as tenderly innocent as love,
as pure and enduring as freedom,
as pregnant with promise as books
is first—to give them away!

To be willing to sacrifice all
for a world still valiantly beating
its way toward beauty, and truth.

May the ash from these fires float free
over all the earth, and all who survive conceive,
be filled, give birth, impart, a love, still, for learning,
a desire for peace everlasting,
a passion to persevere.

* * *

And remember, O Artist, O Poet, remember...*Guernica*—
and look for the answer to war
in art...

MASSACRE AT SREBRENICA (11 July 1995)

Here, six thousand (some say eight)
Bosnian men are mourned.
Rounded up, prodded into fields
they were gunned down like dogs.
Or—*by* dogs, running foxes to the ground,
moving in for the kill?

No, let us not defame the animals. We
are human, *they* are humane. They
would not kill for land, power,
political gain.

After the screaming, shouting,
shooting...how unearthly quiet....

Only the weeping women remain.
Unable to bear the horror, some hang
themselves from trees, their tongues,
eyes bulging out, still
refusing to gaze on a world bereft
of men, home, love, life. Others,
bellies swelling form hunger, disease—
and life from beyond the grave,
form husbands and lovers, fathers children
never shall know.

Where is their safe haven now?
Where can they refugee/go? Sarajevo?
Or to their mass graves there to lie
after the long travail to give birth
to a freedom, a peace, more precious
after the price is paid.

Some few evade their fate by crawling
underneath corpses somehow to hide
from a phantom-democracy not quite yet stillborn,
from the final agony, foresworn for now,
of death of civilization.

WEEDING GRAVES IN A MARTYR'S CEMETERY

In Sarajevo the tombstones are scarred
with bullets. So, too, the still warm bones
in the earth—and the hearts of those
who weep. They come here to mourn
their dead: sons, husbands, lovers, friends.
To sweep the graves, uproot the weeds.
If only they could tear out despair,
destroy the very seeds of destruction
before the war leaves no one to grieve,
above this hard-fought ground.

Truce, peace talks, cease-fire...
Is it too late to save
a world once thought to be
civilized? The cost seems high
to the destitute, starving, bereaved.
Still, our dreams, of a Bosnia
unified, have not died.

SHALOM, AT BITBUG CEMETERY

(And at Bergen-Belsen)

"In the somber wars
of modern democracy
chivalry finds no place."
—Winston Chuchill (1949) *

Our poor bones—
un-shriven, long interred,
cry for remembrance, and peace.
Ah, but there are questions first to ask,
and answer. Must our poor flesh,
awakening too soon
from its hard-earned rest
in Abraham's and this
eternal, earthly breast,
endure forty years and more
of scars weeping afresh?
Are there still enough
tears left unwept?
And must our fathers,
mothers, brothers, sisters,
husbands, wives, children, lovers,
like the poet's ill-starred king
be yet again untimely ripped
from arms, hearts, wombs, tombs,
mocking that insanity
that began on *Kristallnacht?* This
we cannot forget; but must we go on
twisting that two-edged sword
deep in each others' wounds?
Or before too late forgive
somehow, the unforgiveable?
Where and whoever from—such grave
imperatives?—but God! Is this not
His place on earth, His time?
Is love not paramount?

(continuing)

(cont. stanza 1)

Remember, oh remember, whether we
under these lonely few un-mourned headstones lie
or with those countless, nameless other
unmarked, pitiful dead who try to sleep,
we, too, cry to be forgiven if not loved,
if not by one another, then by God
in whose name, image, sight we are, after and
above all, one: German, Jew, and man.

**Ex* "The Ghosts of World War II", George F. Will, *Newsweek,* 29 April 1985. Will's essay stated the moral obligation—in the face of opposition by some Americans, and some Germans, to President Ronald Reagan's proposed visit to Bitburg Cemetery—of victors to honor their slain enemies as well as their own fallen ones.

SHALOM, SHALOM

Muslim Ahmed Khatib, 12, innocent bystander at Israeli-Palestinian street fighting in Jenin, West Bank, died of gunshot on 3 November 2005. In the spirit of *shalom* his organs were given by his family to save Israeli children desperately in need of heart, lung, kidney, liver…*

Peace, in the realm of the abstract,
seems as lofty an ideal as a far-distant star.
And yet, the real word has shone over Earth,
pure, promising pregnant with hope. A Mystery,
lingering on the lips, on the faithful human tongue.
And at Mass we pass along the Kiss of Peace,
delivering each other into God's hands.
Faith, however sown, is uplifting. But where,
ask the psalmists and St. Paul, are our good works,
where our love for our enemies as for ourselves?

There, on the West Bank. Reborn, in lands long torn apart
by wars coldbloodly fought *entr'acte* and re-act.
A gift, Muslim to Israeli, Israel from Palestine. A talisman
of peace, finite yet infinite: one warmly-beating heart.

God's is the great gift of life, truly. And in the end
peace is a gift, humble and serene, that only we
freely and forgivingly can bequeath
to one another.

* (Reported by Scott Wilson in the *Washington, Post* 10 November 2005.
Reprinted in *The Atlanta Journal-Constitution*, 13 November 2005.)

OPERATION DESERT STORM: DESERT STORM REVISITED

And missiles cry herald where once was a Star.

Tonight, the Arabian winds pour over the desert like wine,
bittersweet, clear and cold. And tomorrow? Hot and dry,
sand storms and war bombs. Land of contrasts, extremes.

Our troops are destroying their personal mail
(it's said) for fear those writing may fall
into terrorist hands, into death and hate.

Ah!—but do lovers, and words, ever die?
Though burned to ash beneath canopied skies,
their bitterness-sweetness incensing the air
like prayer? Or buried in sands
that thirst for the blood
of hero and martyr, prophet, Messiah?

Oh if we could but scatter like flowers
more peaceful blooms over desperate nations.
Letters, canticles—Francis's, Paul's.
Sonnets and stanzas and cantos of love.

Once, a century or so ago, there
was such a sonnet written, in England,
an elegy by Oscar Wilde: "On the Sale
by Auction of Keats's Love Letters".
How little we still know, the poet
still seems to say, of what it is we do,
of the mystery of loss and gain
as we lay waste the love
that our hearts for others
gloriously has lain.

But earthly passions wait for the Divine

And peace still seeks such hallowed time
to speak her pure, poetic rhyme.

OPERATION DESERT STORM: THE KISS

Weeping, kneeling, they kiss your hand
even as you capture them, your Iraqi
prisoners of war. Supplicants pressing reverence
upon a bishop's ring, like the Pope's
forgiven assassin's penitent
obeisance to God.

His blood mixed with tears,
the captive in your arms
reaches to kiss your cheek.
Judas kissing Jesus;
Francis embracing the leper,
Placing kisses upon his brow;
Magdalene, anointing Christ's feet
With her tears, drying them with her hair.

"Love your enemies", Jesus said.
But where are they, Marine? When you stare
into your captives' eyes who is there
to look forth upon you, but Christ?

Once a romantic general said
of his desert warrior adversary
I shall send him engraved invitation
in iambic pentameter to join me in battle,
and we two shall decide the fate of the world!

Prisoners, patriots, priests and poets
romanticize war to endure it.
Waging our wars on the battlefield
that lies in the minds of men, beyond
the clashing of symbols, of swords
between two soldiers newly conquered
by an age-old kiss of peace.

OPERATION DESERT STORM: LOVE POEMS OF AN IRAQI SOLDIER

They are in retreat, they have fled
Kuwait, city and state, the Iraqi troops.
Back to horizons obscured: dreams
into ashes, oil into smoke. We can see
their turmoil of parting, shaking
the dust from their feet from this land
burning to be free. Tanks, guns, abandoned,
litter the roads, but a few
treasures, effects paying tribute
to our oneness in dying, our dead.

One of our soldiers stumbles
across a lost journal, it too
casualty of a cruel war
raping its naked pages,
victims, innocent
as birds in withered trees
fishes in blackened seas
creatures and peoples mirrored,
in our foreign, sorrowful eyes,
for these two thousand years.

"The Iraqi poet mourns: "My life
is over, for I am no longer with you."
Still, does he not live? In these
deathless words and the sighs
of his grieving beloved,
as Allah wills?

OPERATION DESERT STORM: SLAUGHTER OF THE INNOCENTS

Peaceful the little one sleeps
into death, her trusting eyes still open,
loath to close even on this harsh world.
Her body already tenderly swathed—
a blanket, not to keep out the cold
but the earth. An infant. How old?
Six months? Twelve? Who can tell
from the small waxen face
aged beyond years like all her clan.
In his vigil for her last breath
her father clutches her tight, his tears
ice in his beard. A bitter night.

Barefoot they crawl up the mountains by thousands,
Kurdish refugees, seeking the line
between Turkey/Iraq. And they die,
two thousand a day, of starvation,
exposure, disease. They flee for their lives
from the tyrant whose hawks in the sky
pursue them like rabbits, though they fight
with the courage of cornered lions.

They are not alone in their suffering.
In the South a Shiite mother in anguish,
swathed in her black mourning robes, her veils,
weeps for the body of her young son
who stumbled upon a land mine, at play.

And what of those other innocents
slaughtered, gassed, cut down—
in Judea, Halabja, Dachau…?
To this day, Herod spares them not.

ARSON IN NORTHERN IRELAND

Ten churches put to the torch make
a fiery pyre where innocence sleeps,
a childhood's bier, a sacred pall,
and bitter tears we can but weep.
All for the sake of a march, parade
sworn to cross a forbidden enclave.
A patriot's statement, you say?
Not a religious one? Perhaps. But acts
that pit faith against faith, flesh
against flesh, fear against fear, are
sacrilege. Mortal, sinful, obscene.
Does not the blood of victims of both
spill warm and red from our common veins—
neither orange nor green? Well, when
will it ever end, then? The violence, pain,
When our guilt is as black as a priest's soutane?
Ah yes—until we confess and begin to hold
the Church, and our souls, sacrosanct.

BREAK-IN IN BELFAST

In Northern Ireland this bitter night
in the midst of the evening meal
terrorists armed with zeal burst in
on a father, mother and offspring, seven.

It's not a religious war
these "patriots" swear, just
a nation a sovereign land
spurning imperial rule.
Protestants, Catholics, victors, victims, all
irrelevant? Past rhyme, reason, belief?
It's purely political, you see.
The children must understand this.
God knows, they've had time to learn.
(but no time for a farewell kiss)

"Daddy, don't die!", the youngest one cries.
God knows he never wanted to, their father.
Had he lived he might have succeeded
in teaching them other ideals, philosophies
other than hate. But those lessons,
unlike death, must wait.

His crimes? Pity—for British soldiers;
compassion; an impulse to compromise,
to forgive his enemies. A credo
to live and die by.

CHAOS IN KOSOVO

I. THE REFUGEES

> "Haziz Shaquiri's wife, son, and daughter...froze to death n a snowstorm while t trying to follow a mountain pass to safety in Macedonia."
>
> — Charles Holmes, Staff Correspondent,
> in *The Atlanta Journal-Constitution*

You—Albanian...Kosovar—hiding there, in your
pastoral sanctuary, once-Arcadian hills,
mountains, woods, trees arched high
like Gothic cathedrals, ancient, inviolate, pure.
Turned back from the border is this your refuge
from hunger, thirst, cold and despair? Overhead
the attacking Apaches dance in midair
over Serbian tanks, troops on the grounds,
while weeping you stare at the fire and the ash
that were your villages, homes, your dead.

We the free world will rescue you
from your genocidal plight,
send medicine, food, water, supplies.
We'll bind up your wounds and anoint you
with our theories just war and unjust,
(while our missiles still rain down)
our pragmatic/democratic/diplomatic ideals,
laborious though they seem
safeguarding human rights.

Are we only innocent dreamers?
Idealists...fools...naive?
Embracing you—*and* your enemy—
with our noble intellectual views
(while our bombs keep raining down)
to repudiate hatred and death,
trying to meet halfway
on some peaceful common ground
our transcendent ideology, *Love.*

CHAOS IN KOSOVO

II. THE CHILDREN

> "An ethnic Albanian girl grasps a barbed wire fence after arriving Tuesday at a NATO-run camp in Stenkovec, Macedonia."
>
> — Marcia Kunstel, Staff Correspondent,
> in *The Atlanta Journal-Constitution,* 18 April 1999

Shrouded in fear in the camps they peer
through veils of barbed wire, bewildered.
Are they better off inside—or out?
Forced back from uncertain borders
from questionable neighboring states,
are they fated to wander the earth
like the twelve tribes dispersed—
or used as human shields?
The life they knew has vanished,
the home to which they may never return.

Appalled, we look on from our insular distance.
Where is their lost childhood's innocence,
their trust in the world that is their inheritance?
Will it ever return? If not, then, the cost
will be too high and the world,
and we, will be poorer. These
are our children, the spoils of war.

CHAOS IN KOSOVO

III. THE CHURCH

> "The Serbian Orthodox Church is part of the Orthodox Christian Church. The Orthodox Church of the East and the Roman Catholic Church split in the Great Schism in 1054. The two groups share basic tenets, but the Orthodox do not follow the pope. Eastern churches follow the Julian calendar, while Western churches use the Gregorian."
>
> — Julia Lieblich, Associated Press,
> in *The Atlanta Journal-Constitution,* 10 April 1999

On Easter, in Rome, the holiest day
of the Christian Gregorian calendar,
the pope urges peace: *Urbi et Orbi.*
his perennial paschal appeal.
Only he and his flock believe
their two-thousand-year faith will see
the new Millennium. Here, in Kosovo
his words, like Christ's, fall on deaf ears.
But still, Tu es Petrus,
Your faith will endure.

Easter, still and again, one week
later, Orthodox Julian time.
The metropolitan, too, adjures
both sides to forgo the fight
on this day of the Lord's Rebirth.

So soldiers geared to kill light candles
at Mass in Belgrade their prayers rising
incensed from earth to listening heaven,
and outside the air raid sirens begin
tolling their lamentations and praise.

CHAOS IN KOSOVO

IV. THE POET

> "About 1,000 Belgrade citizens came out Wednesday to bury Slavko Curyjiva, in independent publisher who was assassinated Sunday."
>
> — Stephen Erlanger, in *The New York Times*
> reprinted in *The Atlanta Journal-Constitution,*
> 15 April 1999

In Belgrade free speech is verboten.
Our editors-publishers die young.
Guns have silenced the printed word.
Journalists are expelled,
peacekeepers long-since banned,
and foreign observers anathema.
You analysts knowing the answer
to war must tell us from afar.

Who now remains to speak/to be heard
for the young, the old, refugees?
Our men are seized and slain,
our women beaten and raped,
mothers, infants cast forth
on their own Flight into Egypt.
How many will ever return
to this holy, expatriate land?

Who, then, is left but the poet
to cry out in loud voice, to warn
that lessons unlearned from the past
are doomed to be repeated?

GEORGIA BOUND—A Confederate Soldier's Soliloquy

...The War's Over! And I, who scarcely dared
count my own life among the spoils of war,
am called by God to live—and love—again!
A few more weary days should see me home.
My name is George and Georgian I was born
as Georgian thought to die, yet I am spared
while all around me braver comrades fall.
Not that I lacked brute courage for the fray—
I rushed into the battle with the rest;
but I have no love for war, killing, death....
Dear God! I know I shall not soon forget
our first duel of death—my "enemy" and I:
God willed I had no brothers of my own;
yet he, bewildered by my Rebel yell—
before my rifle ball profaned his breast—
was more my brother than if Georgia born.
I wished I'd kissed his hand before he died;
I wish I had my brother back again.
(Yank, when we meet again, please be my friend!)
I feel no shame in longing to find peace,
knowing now that war's more wrong than right—
as once I thought it honorable to fight.
But who knows what I'll find as I journey home?
Has Sherman put the torch to Milledgeville?
Does Vickie watch—or sleep on Memory Hill?
The War is Lost! And yet my dreams still ride
Northward to Virginia with Doles and Lee!
Never have troops had greater guides to war—

(continuing)

(cont. stanza 1)

who nobly paid their debts to God and man
yet, while they spent just anger on the foe,
taught us to love our enemies as men.
And so, although the South has lost the battle,
please God we've won the war of man for man.
For as we sprang from such courageous forebears,
we must bear seeds of even braver men
who'll teach their sons never again to lay,
like Cain on Abel, brother's hand on hand…
to hear no more the screams of dying men
forever now beyond our recompense,
except the telling that—now—we love them well,
for we, too, learned the self-mockery of hate.
These are my thoughts as Georgia bound I plod-
Homeward, ever homeward—to thee, O God….

DIASPORA

Today, in Somalia, in South Africa,
a mother and child lie at rest
in the dust of a modern *diaspora*
in the ash of a new holocaust.

Piteous walking wraiths
thin lost remnants of thousands
traversing hundreds of miles seeking
life from a raped, ravaged land,
empty food bowls in hand.

Anarchy, looting, civil war the jackboots
trampling this sacrosanct threshold
between breath and death. As if
divine acts can be outshone.
Governments gone, guns
laws of their own, famine
from withered crops, hunger
swelling their bellies, flies
weighing their spirits, eyes, thirst-
cursed drought driving them on
they wander the barren plains
sustained only by hope.

Dispossessed, they return to earth
more than they ever took from it:
humility, nobility, Giving up
the ghost their no longer living
skeletons stilled, their flesh-
stretched bones now to lie
shrouded in bits of cloth
bound for waiting graves,
stacked like bundles of sticks
to light that fire consuming
all but their souls; to go free.

Soon the rains will come
chilling their nakedness
the final, fateful touch
of exposure and disease.

(continuing)

(begin stanza 6)

Desolate mothers press their young
to their shrunken, shriveling breasts.
When their milk, too, thins and dries
they will die in each other's arms.
Children crying, dying in silence
too old ever to know their youth,
parents softly wailing their grief
hoping to live long enough
only to bury their dead.

Lives offered up, laid down
hundreds by night by day
slaves to ground and sky
subject only to hope,
Spent, starved, they wait
at the very gates of the camp
for some dreamed-of kiss of welcome
to life, not death.

Will that kiss be too little too late
for this mother, this child?
This baby not too far gone
playfully, shyly to smile,
hiding all but one
trusting, questioning eye?
So may it have seemed, before,
for that other Mother and Child.
Resting, on the flight into Egypt,
at the whim of kings, at the will of God.

Is there hope? Perhaps.
As the tribal warlords pause,
to sound their truce, perhaps
Herod the Great is no more.

And if not? Ah, then, perchance
Somalia's poets may find,
as in Spain's *Guernica*,
the ultimate expression of pain
and answer to war...in art.

THE JAIN TEMPLE

An Ode to Brotherhood

Once I stood transfixed, timid American tourist that I was,
innocent, naive voyager-around-the-world, finding myself
with my more worldly husband/soul-mate in the midst
of India's exotic, overwhelming city of poverty and wealth,
Mumbai (Bombay), hesitant but privileged, bare of foot, to enter
the *sanctum sanctorum* of an impressive Jain temple.

At the time, I knew nothing, or little, of the Far East,
less of Asian/Indian faiths: Buddhist, Muslim, Hindu,
their diverse cults, sects and dialects. Our friendly Parsi
tour guide spoke mainly (in good English, not in Farsi)
of pride in her own heritage and customs—some seeming,
to our enlightened Western minds and tastes, quite unrefined.

The temple, a life-like elephant greeting us outside, was colorful,
airy, open to the street, thronged with ardent Jain celebrants
murmuring prayers, lighting candles and fragrant incense, and with
our cruise ship travel mates, seeking new diversions in the wake
of an anti-U.S. port of call passed by. India's warm welcome, then, seemed
to meet our Anglo-Saxon need to be universally esteemed (our idle dream!).

Only later, on the threshold of a new millennium, as yet unaware of coming terror and of war,
I sensed something in myself struggling to be born—a philosophy, an ideal, ever green:
respect, and love, for not only God and man but the whole natural world,
all living breathing growing things of whatever size and state, great and small.
Awed by revelation, I found myself in harmony, Jain in thought and ways
with that most gracious company of His, and Nature's, humblest devotees.
Sweeping the ground before my feet lest unseeing and unfeeling I deprive one human soul,
or any other God-given breath of life on earth, its hope to by-pass death, its right to survive.
Discovering that we, so absolute in our Judeo-Christian mystery, our passionate, inviolate
Catholic conviction of the *essence* of our Faith, may not, *otherwise*, be so different after all
from all other cultures, peoples, strife-worn lands—from any/every other sacred and serene,
all-embracing, peaceful and non-violent, Creator-and-Creation-graced, body of belief.

NESCIT CEDERE *

(for James Edward Oglethorpe, 1696-1785, and
in honor of the University that bears his name)

Brave General—still, as Georgians, we reflect
your faith in debtors longing to be free.
Our debt—to you—through George *secundus, rex*,
is one we strive to pay most faithfully.
Founder…father…our history never palls!
Without your tireless vigor would we still—
Upon this sacred soil, these grounds, these halls—
Uphold our God, who teaches all His will?
Heroic, gallant, and—above all—just,
Through you we raise our living monument,
unfailing in our sacredness of trust
to honor you, with triumphs still unspent.
"…People unborn thy merits shall proclaim…."
So we, with Pope, pay tribute to your name.

("He does not know how to give up"* –from General Oglethorpe's Coat of Arms)

(Alexander Pope's lines on Oglethorpe:

"Hail, Oglethorpe! With nobler triumphs crowned
Than ever were in camps or sieges found—
Thy great example shall through ages shine,
A fav'rite theme with poet and divine;
People unborn they merits shall proclaim,
And add new honors to thy deathless name.")

(quoted in EVANS, Lawton B.: *A History of Georgia* (for use in Schools), State History Series. American Book Company, New York, 1908, pp. 37-38)

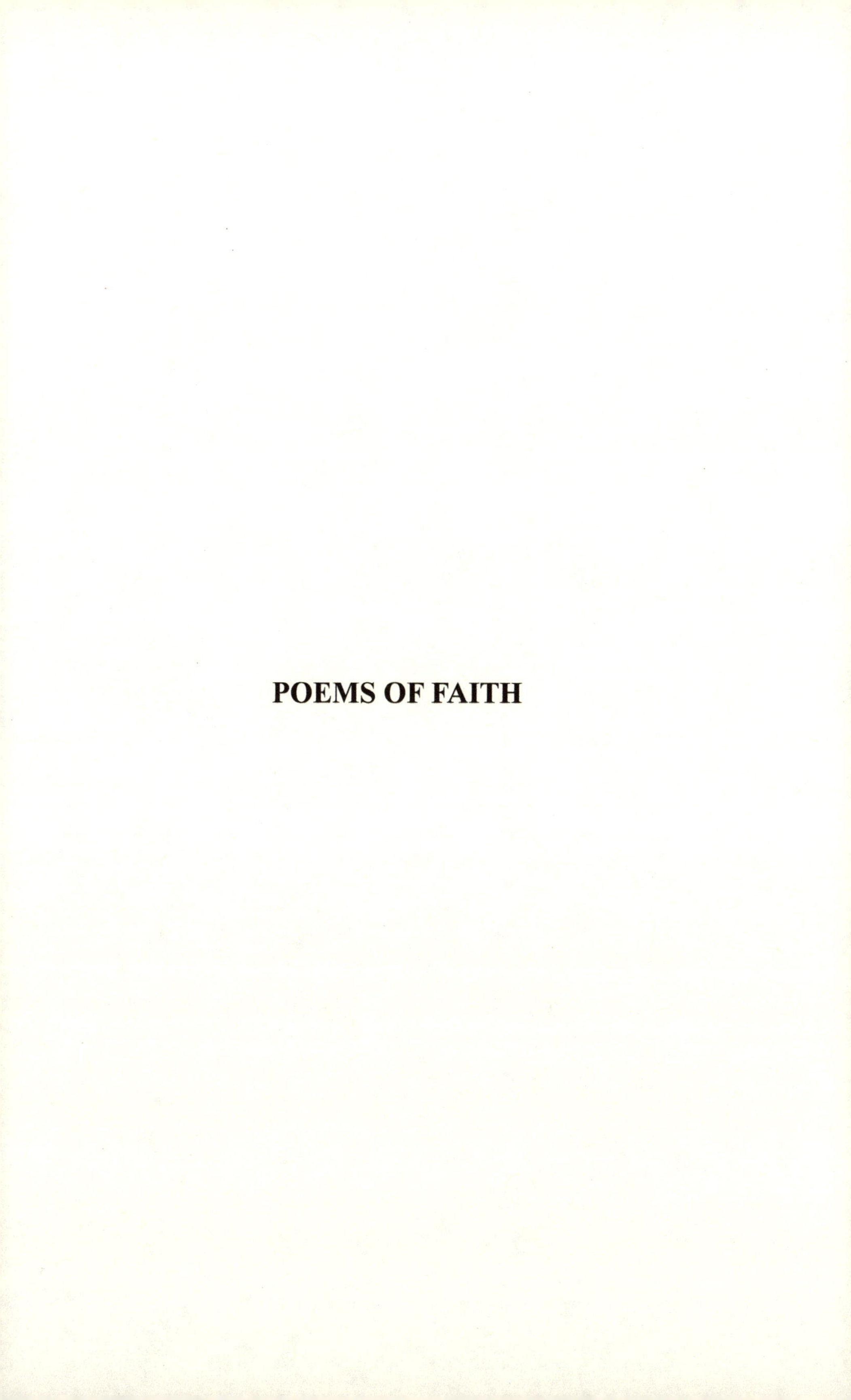

POEMS OF FAITH

THE VEIL

Embracing the Faith is like falling,
they say, in love—with God, and man.
I know, I know! In what less glorious
passionate state dare we even dream
of such a symmetry, so tenuous, tender,
and true? God knows, the divine Passion
pales all others under the sun.
The rending of that Templed veil
top to bottom, darkness from light
turns night into day, and love to Love.
And still, but still, you and I dream
we, too, love one another enough
to part all the distances lying between us,
to lay bare our mysteries, spirit and heart.

FOR AN UNKNOWN DISFIGURED ONE (In The Cathedral)

As yet you do not know
I've come to claim you for my own
as someone dear to love
to pray for,
someone to love.

How could you?
You barely meet my eye when I
pause sometimes to greet you;
but, then, I too am shy.

The superficial fact
that you've been somewhat disfigured by,
like St. Francis, great affliction,
does not matter.

That only means, I believe,
that really means you are beloved,
greatly so by God,
and so, by me.

I only wish I had the courage to reach higher,
like St. Francis, to kiss your ravaged brow—
as he enthroned his lonely lepers;
to say how much I need you
to love and pray for me
to tell you you are infinitely
more beautiful than I.

ADVENT

The Church in the heart of the city
is a lake in a perishing land,
an oasis waiting at the end
of a cold, wind-swept street.
Home for the otherwise homeless,
Bread and Wine for the starving,
a feast, a vision of hope for those
whose eyes will come to see.

And for me, for me?—a flame
of love burning to lighten,
Heart to heavy heart,
even the darkest night.

KNEELING WITH POPE JULIUS IN THE SISTINE CHAPEL

Against all the very best
custom and convention,
our arbitrary rules
of creative force and form,
I kneel before your scaffold
looking upward, ever upward
with Pope Julius, admiring
but impatient, still to grasp
all you have brought forth
of Creation and of Judgment
by a gesture of your hand
in the flutter of an eye.

Oh I'm with you, but in spirit;
in Spirit, Michelangelo—
only dreaming I am near you
in the Chapel where you are.
That I speak of you at all
in my unstudied state and fashion
seems proof I must move nearer,
with you, to truth and art,
and that I too must learn the rules
before I dare to break the rules:
to paint, with brush or pen,
what I have not seen.

MENDICANT BEFORE THE CHURCH OF ST. DENIS

Midway a wide step to the high façade
she reclines, a beggar-girl clutching
what I take to be a bundle of rags.
Then surprised I see it is a child,
a baby, an infant not long from the womb.
Staring, stunned, I shrink, draw back,
pondering how/if she will suckle him.
here and now to make their plight
more pitiable still to passers-by—
tourists, such as my husband and I.

Three days in Athens this is our first
glimpse of the poor great cities know
in bold encounters/meetings of Old
World and New. Has she a license to beg,
I wonder, as in our native U.S.
Is the child even hers?—or merely one
borrowed to flesh out a *verismo* tableau?
Her palm outstretched my husband blesses
with a few Greek coins, and I know shame
for my own poverty of compassion.

What had I dreamed, Aegean-bound—
that truth is beauty, beauty truth,
with no pall cast by the specter of want?
Yet who is lovelier, richer than she?—
Pale as her marble sarcophagus,
warmed by a golden, Attic sun.
The Acropolis crowned by the Parthenon.
Timeless. Eternal. But now it's time
to light a candle, celebrate a rite,
confess our sins, do what we must.

CARAVANSERAI

Oh yes, it is hard
not to believe, as I
only astrally wandering lie
by my bedroom window
this starlit midnight pondering
how near they seem or are the stars
philosophic romantic mystic
dreamer that I am,
in caravans and stanzas of stars
crossing the heavens foretold
to light some traveler's way.

Is it star, or poet, so moved?

Remember that fabled Star
of the East? And the Stable
on which it shone? Can it be
all but they are fixed, still,
and afar? Ah then, say it is we,
you and I, dazzling Dante's stars
and traversing Empyrean skies
to our fated rendezvous.

ANNUNCIATION

Last night I awoke from sleeping,
from falling asleep in the midst
of the first Joyful Mystery:
trying, failing, to stay awake
to pray, my rosary still in hand.

Yet, no sooner asleep than awakened
as if by light—radiant, streaming
its warm benediction over me,
that cold, clear midnight nearing
the dawn of Our Savior's birth.

Oh, the refreshing wonder of waking
as though by roses playfully shaken!
Or holy water lightly flinging.
A sprinkling of stars, perhaps,
brushed by an angel's wing?

Was it thus you were awakened,
Mary, O Most Blessèd Mother?
In awed, half-sleeping joy receiving
that most dreamlike salutation
from the Presence that is Real?

CHOICES

(reverie, by the yet-to-be-born)

I...who am become
the soul of papal decree,
symbol of argument for
choices pro and con,
serene eye of the storm
of the sea of controversy
upon whose swelling breast
my brief, uncertain spirit
rests—a game of chance
toying with my existence,
tossing it on the tides
of our unjointed times...
seem, withal, of small moment to
a world that only half welcomes
me, bloodied but unbowed.
Oh, but do they know
what I might yet become.
What other limits are there
but God's laws, commands
graced by faith to be
upheld or cast down
by men on men?
He knows and overthrows
the odds against me,
all the prevailing winds
and waves. I'm human,
true, and of this earth,
but divinely made!
The last faint breath
of conscience to be heard.
The test of life and love.
And you who fear nothing,
daring to toy with the atoms,
are you not, still,
in awe of me?

CREDO

Credo, perche—
even in this modern world
of conspicuous consumption
and instant gratification,
of lust passing for love,
and repudiation of life
a compulsion to death, still
it is hard *not* to believe!

Credo, because
I reject the fruits of unbelief—
chaos, despair, banishment
from You, O Lord.

I believe, because
This our world still is one
of infinite grace and beauty,
of passion and compassion,
of faithfulness and Faith,
and of creativeness—
of books, music, poetry, art
that, like Love and Life,
are deathless.

Two thousand years we've knelt before You,
beside Your artists, poets, saints:
Francis, Dante, Michelangelo....
All those who, too, embraced You
against the chaos of their times.

(continuing)

(begin stanza 5)

We are still made in Your image, Lord,
and You are still clothed in our humanness.
Stay with us then, we pray,
that we may not turn away
from our still pure and child-like love
for beauty that is eternal,
for the Presence that is Real—
for You, O Lord.

So we go on believing
in the good that surely still must lie
deep in the heart of every man.
We are every man, but You, Lord, are, still,
the beating Heart and Soul of things.

INSOMNIA IN THE GRAVE

And what if one should be
insomniac in the grave?
Is it not hard enough to ponder
ways to pass the time here on earth,
let alone beneath it? Counting sheep—
or measured rhymes—an hour or two
some sleepless night, is one thing,
but a hundred years, a century,
millennium, an aeon or two—is not
the thought itself enough
to affright the bravest soul's
mind's eye with certain dread?
Shakespeare said it best: *"To die,*
to sleep, perchance to dream..." And yet
who would not rather dream
than lie awake while mind, heart race
like King Richard's ghosts' hastening
to cast upon uneasy consciences
all that one has done and left undone
in thought, word and deed, on earth?
To sleep…to dream…to lie at rest….
Who can choose? Better to take
what comes, not tremble
in fear of some unknown,
and patiently await
the outcome of God's plan
for man.

ON VISITING THE TOMB OF A REVERED WRITER, IN IRAKLION, CRETE

"I believe in nothing, I hope for nothing, I am free"
—Nikos Kazantzakis (1885-1959) (epitaph)

Ah, Nikos, what do they mean, your enigmatic words?
You—who wrote on the great themes and men
of flesh and spirit: Zorba, Francis, and Christ.
Cause of your own excommunion, mystifying
your Church above all, your words of such
terrible beauty and cost—like Michelangelo's
terribilità. What has it cost you, your genius,
wrung from your very soul?

I believe, *credo*, that no one, no one—unless
he has so loved this world, with your passionate Greek soul,
so loved your beautiful Crete, upon whose bosom you lie,
has crept so tenderly into the heart of your sainted subject Francis,
so wrestled like Jacob with God, to reconcile God with man,
and yet, and yet, has simply *loved* God *and* man—
can write with such magnificence,
having learned, truly at last, to "transubstantiate":
to take that matter God has given us
and turn it into spirit.

Homer and Kazantzakis—brave, heroic
as one in your epic earthly odysseys:

> *"In middle of the sable sea there lies*
> *An isle called Crete, a ravisher of eyes...."*

(continuing)

(begin stanza 5)

(O fruitful Crete!—of olives and grapes and poets)

I do believe in life you believed/hoped much
and revel now only in freedom
from that great struggle we lose only to God.
The stones of your tomb are as strong as your heart.
The Cross guarding your grave is eternal.
And so we leave you to Heaven.

Peace, Nikos, Peace.

THE SUM OF THINGS

What poet does not fear the end death brings
to art, and still—unspent by time or fate—
his last undying poem would create?
Like Francis, poet-saint, would he not wing
more eagerly to heaven if to sing
such verses there to win God's laureate?
Of such a heaven poets dream!—and wait
for Dante's stars to write the sum of things.

Some say that God and poets (if they're true)
alone create. And once perfection came
on earth. Pray then, poet, that such a God
will yet send such a One as Christ for you,
your perfect poem in paradise to claim.
For what on earth can rhyme with God, but God?

TO A PALSIED ONE CLIMBING THE STEPS OF THE CATHEDRAL

We meet here this morning quite by chance
at the base of the steps of the Cathedral.
You pass me, lunging up the hill,
intent upon your urgent goal,
unable to heed my tentative greeting.
But our glances, like our purposes, cross.
I wonder and yet do not at your hurry
though it is but twelve,
the next Mass at half past.
Some may think your haste occasioned
by your infirmity, the unsteadiness
of your gait, your flailing members
possessing seemingly wills of their own,
contrary to your determined direction.
But undeterred, undistracted, slowly
you haul yourself up the stairs.
Ten minutes or more it is taking you
clutching the guard rail leading upward.
And I, too, need more time to climb
the Cathedral steps; the way is steep.

A young boy, thin, too pale, perhaps twenty,
too painfully wrenched into life, into manhood
but plainly anxious to pay the price.
Your body already above and beyond me,
your eyes well-fixed on their reason for eagerness
to receive and make, to again partake
of that far from passive sacrifice.

(continuing)

(cont. stanza 2)

The day is so chill—dark, and raining;
no wonder our thoughts precede us inside
to the comfort of light, the warm consolation
of the one place body and soul can be whole,
can be reconciled wholly; there where, kneeling,
our tremulous frenzy is finally stilled.
I follow, bemused, not quite catching up
though longing to meet your satisfied gaze,
reflecting more deeply our mystery, vision
of seeing <u>Him</u>, then, look forth from us both,
to see there confirmed our humble conviction
that our presence too is urgently needed,
that now, at last, the Mass may begin.

CENTERING

Stare into the center of the sun
and wonder at its leaping
wildly side to side as though
tempted to depart its boundaries—
or reveling in its limits circumscribed.

Unlike Lucifer the earth
in its brief shining morning hour
toying with the idea of rebellion
against all natural order
of creation—pauses
at the edge of anarchy, before
daring to war with stars
that, too, may fade and fall.

Will it center itself in time?
Like art? To a measured rhyme?

Stare at the center of the sun
and it dances, as Fatima!
As the prophet leapt for joy
when the circle was complete.

FOR STEPHANIE, WHO CRIED FOR BREAD

You were only three and a half today,
my companion at noontime Mass,
just becoming acquainted with
the world outside, the world within.

Composed, beside me, patiently waiting
with a crayon or two, a book (unread),
perusing instead the windows, statues,
images: Jesus, Mary, and the saints.

Until I went to partake of Christ...
Expectantly, part of me, close in line,
eagerly keeping your hand in mine—
then denied, heart breaking, you cried.

"But I <u>wanted</u> one," you said,
(with all our human thwarted passion)
lips trembling, lashes starred
with tears I'm sure will flower in heaven!

Later—good humor restored, on your knees,
eyes twinkling, hands clasped, copying me—
I mused: was "O God, make me good (but not yet!)"
your mischievous, Franciscan/Augustinian plea?

And how soon, dear chosen one, will you know
you were crying for so much more than bread?

RECONSTRUCTED THOUGHTS ON DELIVERANCE AND RESURRECTION

A tribute in honor of Bernard Bryan,
one of 24 courageous survivors of the Atlanta plane crash—
Southern Flight 242, New Hope, Georgia, 4 April 1977—
and in memory of the 70 brave souls who perished,
to deliver their own psalms of praise to God
in His presence.

I.

* <u>I will lift up mine eyes unto the hills.</u>
<u>from whence cometh my help.</u>

Is ever mankind's faith in man—and God—
Put to a more devastating test
Than in the aftermath of tragedy:
Of an unforeseen, near-fatal airplane crash?
What were my thoughts as I and eighty-four
other beings, created in His image,
Hung suspended in that infinity
That might've held our last sweet breath of life,
Our last sweet, wondering memory of this word?
How can I say?...still scarcely can I think!
To reconstruct the terror is (almost)
Quite as terrible as living through it.

(<u>O Lord!</u> Thy world is beautiful—so dear!
How can we then deny thy presence here?)

II.

* <u>My help cometh from the Lord,</u>
<u>which made heaven and earth.</u>

For one brief hour the plane becomes my world—
All its inhabitants my fellow men,
Linked together by pre-destination
And by our welcome fantasy-escape
From worldly care and every earthly need.
Enough to be transported here-to-there,
Lulled by the stewardesses tending bar,
Secure in the dynamics of air flight,
The skill of crew on ground and in the sky;
And—dulled to that most real reality
that secretly upholds my sacred hopes:
Belief in God (so soon to be invoked).

(<u>O Lord</u>! Yet though I wander far from thee,
I know that thou shall ever follow me!)

III.

* <u>He will not suffer thy foot to be moved:</u>
<u>he that keepeth thee will not slumber.</u>

How awesome is the tempest, suddenly!
One instant we fly free, so clear and fair,
The next stalled in the chilling flame-out
Of jet-age power and self-complacency—
Our wing tips knighted by a lightning sword,
Crowned and baptized by such cascading pearls

As hailstones of unprecedented size,
Christening us who are to be reborn
"Children of God" (we few, we chosen few!),
Anointing others their last rites of doom.
And now we're struck with equal awe that we,
Fearing we're not immortal, long to be!

(O Lord! Thy storm is wonderful and wild,
and by its very force we are beguiled!)

IV.

* Behold, he that keepeth Israel
shall neither slumber nor sleep.

In this last, private, precious moment
Of truth and unassimilated dread,
My faith in the sovereignty of Man—
Within, upon, above his planet Earth—
Pales beneath my dawning faith in God.
But the pilots are magnificent! Calm,
Contained, in their self-disciplined assurance
That practice to perfection alone brings,
They follow the prescribed ritual
Of the science of their high aspiring art
That may still yield (if all its principles
Are properly applied?) our safe return.

(O Lord! We pray they mercy on us all
that it may be thy will we shall not fall!)

V.

* The Lord is thy keeper:
the lord is thy shade upon thy right hand.

Then what went wrong? Where ever did we err?
Nothing; everywhere! Can the hand of Man
Outreach the mighty arm and act of God?
With luck (some say) we might have made it,
Had the road been wider to receive us
And had the trees, the trees, been not so tall!
But the earth was waiting to bequeath us
Her last embrace of sweet mortality:
We seventy...burned and bleeding, bare and bruised souls!
Oh God, oh God, I cried, am I deserving
To live because men (too!) have lived and died—
By sacrifice redeeming my salvation?

(O Lord! Now fill us with thy loving breath
as we the living try to succor death!)

VI.

* The sun shall not smite thee by day,
nor the moon by night.

For I—I am one of but two dozen,
four and twenty resurrected souls
Who somewhere, sometime, somehow merited
Or earned the grace to live and love again.
But how, my Lord, shall I prove worthy
Of this thy gift of love and life restored?

And this my joy in being rejoined to those
Who wept lest I be lost to them forever?
Perhaps—by cherishing this happiness...
This sweet foreshadowing of Heavenly bliss?
For I—I am delivered now from Hell
To tell of God's impassioned love for Man!

(O Lord! I am so small—and though so grand;
yet thou has held me, held me, in thy hand!)

VII.

* The Lord shall preserve thee from all evil:
he shall preserve thy soul.

Is it life's survivors who have risen?
Or death's "victims" who have, truly, been delivered?
Please God I may, some day, find the answer
To the airplane's homeward-struggling runway
To our rendezvous with destiny.
As my own yearning soul may one day too,
God willing, rejoin its source and goal.
How strange!—I never really understood before
This joyous Pesach/joyful Easter season
Of tragedy most bitter/sweetest triumph,
Man's human passion to believe divine
Both his Deliverance and his Resurrection!

(O Lord!—God of our fathers and of Man—
Thus may all men praise thy almighty plan!)

* The Lord shall preserve thy going out and thy coming in,
from this time forth, and even for evermore.

TRIPTYCH

GOD TO ADAM TO EVE

In my desire and intent to possess you
to encompass all that you are
and will ever be, to me
to reclaim all that I've given
so gladly, so generously
to share life's goodness with you
to someday return it to me
perhaps I am too overwhelming
too eager to fill and consume you
at the table I've joyfully laid
so joyously spread before you.
You, too, are starving, I know
almost as insatiate as I
for the essence of truth and of beauty.
I know, I know you desire me
and would be forever possessed
but have patience, forebear in the midst
at the height of the banquet of plenty
and until I know you are ready
to love me above all others
to receive all I would give you
in knowledge of good not evil
do not partake too importunely
of life's sweet, arboreal secret
but thoughtfully, gently, belovèd
prolonging our idyll of joy.

TRIPTYCH

ADAM TO EVE

Perhaps I frighten you
in my eagerness
to possess you?
(and to be so possessed)
Perhaps I'm too overwhelming
and my passion itself too new
in our new
(now, with you)
Paradise.
God knows *I'm* overwhelmed
by the feast here
spread before me
by the table so
sumptuously laid.
Eat, drink, God said
(knowing my hunger, my thirst)
of none but one I deny you.
But *you* are not forbidden me
nor I to you, my love
so be not uncertain or fearful
in your pretended
or real naïveté
for you are Woman!—
already no doubt full of knowing
what I barely but eagerly sense:
that I'm destined to be your slave!

TRIPTYCH

EVE TO ADAM TO GOD

I'm awed—to the depths of my being.
You're so beautiful, strong, and wise,
But I never, never could fear you
for there's tenderness in your eyes.
I would, rather, be filled with anguish
to ever bring grief to you
for I love you so much already
I would eagerly, quickly conceive
of some way to return, and earn
your gift of life ot me.
I want so much to believe
all that you whisper to me
even that guilt is not yet
and that it need never be.
Though you've given me bone flesh and breath
and received my heart in return
as you say, I am Woman, born knowing
perhaps more than Man ever can
that in loving, before we can win
as in living, there's so much to lose.
Forgive me then please, my love
if it's I who ever betray you
for, still, I am flesh of your flesh
and will ever be bone of your bone
as you are my Lord in Heaven
and, forever, lord of my earth.

AFTERWORLD

And what was it like to lose
you, my world from afar?
What can I say?—but that the moon
that caught its light in your eyes
became dark. And the sun
that warmed us as we grew old
grew cold. And oceans, tides
that pulled us together froze.
And the stars we aspired to
fell from the skies. Otherwise
Earth still spins on its axis,
I still read and write, and
you, so near to me, still
turn prose into poetry.

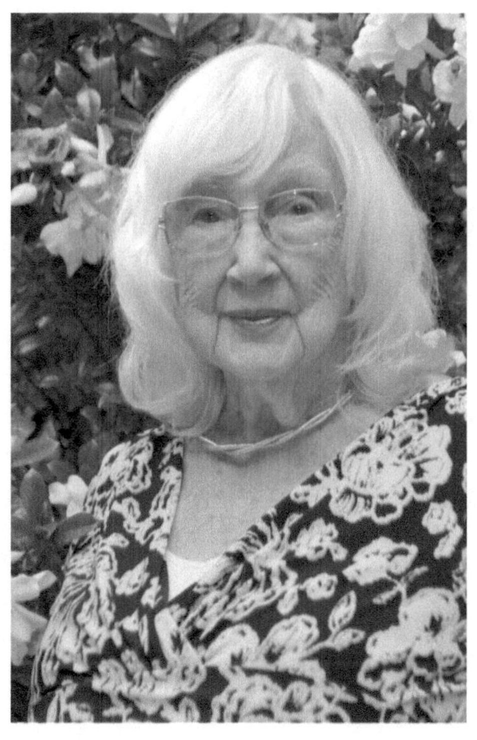

ABOUT THE AUTHOR

Patricia Anne Kirby Craddock was born in Atlanta, Georgia. Graduate of The Academy of St. Genevieve-of-the-Pines in Asheville, North Carolina, she attended Georgia State College for Women (Milledgeville) and Oglethorpe University. A founding member of the Georgia State Poetry Society, she is a member of the Poetry Society of America and the Academy of American Poets. In 1982, she was elected a Life Fellow of the International Academy of Poets, Cambridge, England.

www.ingramcontent.com/pod-product-compliance
Lightning Source LLC
LaVergne TN
LVHW091046080826
845145LV00002B/639

* 9 7 8 0 9 9 1 3 0 0 9 2 1 *